Rethinking Peace and Conflict Studies

Series Editors
Oliver P. Richmond, University of Manchester, Manchester, UK
Annika Björkdahl, Department of Political Science, Lund University, Lund, Sweden
Gëzim Visoka, Dublin City University, Dublin, Ireland

This agenda-setting series of research monographs, now more than a decade old, provides an interdisciplinary forum aimed at advancing innovative new agendas for peace and conflict studies in International Relations. Many of the critical volumes the series has so far hosted have contributed to new avenues of analysis directly or indirectly related to the search for positive, emancipatory, and hybrid forms of peace. Constructive critiques of liberal peace, hybrid peace, everyday contributions to peace, the role of civil society and social movements, international actors and networks, as well as a range of different dimensions of peace (from peacebuilding, statebuilding, youth contributions, photography, and many case studies) have been explored so far. The series raises important political questions about what peace is, whose peace and peace for whom, as well as where peace takes place. In doing so, it offers new and interdisciplinary perspectives on the development of the international peace architecture, peace processes, UN peacebuilding, peacekeeping and mediation, statebuilding, and localised peace formation in practice and in theory. It examines their implications for the development of local peace agency and the connection between emancipatory forms of peace and global justice, which remain crucial in different conflict-affected regions around the world. This series' contributions offer both theoretical and empirical insights into many of the world's most intractable conflicts, also investigating increasingly significant evidence about blockages to peace.

This series is indexed by Scopus.

Brendan Ciarán Browne

Transitional (in)Justice and Enforcing the Peace on Palestine

Brendan Ciarán Browne
Trinity College Dublin
Belfast, Ireland

ISSN 1759-3735　　　　　　ISSN 2752-857X　(electronic)
Rethinking Peace and Conflict Studies
ISBN 978-3-031-25393-5　　　ISBN 978-3-031-25394-2　(eBook)
https://doi.org/10.1007/978-3-031-25394-2

© The Author(s), under exclusive license to Springer Nature Switzerland AG 2023
This work is subject to copyright. All rights are solely and exclusively licensed by the Publisher, whether the whole or part of the material is concerned, specifically the rights of translation, reprinting, reuse of illustrations, recitation, broadcasting, reproduction on microfilms or in any other physical way, and transmission or information storage and retrieval, electronic adaptation, computer software, or by similar or dissimilar methodology now known or hereafter developed.
The use of general descriptive names, registered names, trademarks, service marks, etc. in this publication does not imply, even in the absence of a specific statement, that such names are exempt from the relevant protective laws and regulations and therefore free for general use.
The publisher, the authors, and the editors are safe to assume that the advice and information in this book are believed to be true and accurate at the date of publication. Neither the publisher nor the authors or the editors give a warranty, expressed or implied, with respect to the material contained herein or for any errors or omissions that may have been made. The publisher remains neutral with regard to jurisdictional claims in published maps and institutional affiliations.

Cover illustration: © Harvey Loake

This Palgrave Macmillan imprint is published by the registered company Springer Nature Switzerland AG
The registered company address is: Gewerbestrasse 11, 6330 Cham, Switzerland

For Emma.

Preface

It's the 17th of November 2015 and I am sitting in a small room on the Bard College campus at the Al Quds University, located in the Jerusalem suburb of Abu Dis. In a few minutes, I will begin another class on international law and transitional justice. Enrolled in the module are students who will have travelled from towns, cities, and refugee camps across Palestine, including Ramallah, Hebron, Nablus, Tulkarem, Abu Dis, Jerusalem, and Bethlehem. Since the semester began in August, there has been a discernible rise in what some commentators routinely (and incorrectly) reference as 'tensions' and 'clashes', with several suggesting that we may be witnessing the beginning of a 'third' ('knife') Intifada. As a result, the journey to class for my students, always difficult, violent, and time-consuming, has become more dislocated and unpredictable than normal. Messages soon begin to drop into my mailbox explaining that the 'container' checkpoint is closed; a heavily militarised space controlled by the Israeli army and its security subcontractors, located at the top of *Wadi Al Nar*, in the heart of the occupied West Bank. No-one is being allowed through and several *services* (small minibuses) are turning back. Others send messages via Facebook asking: 'Hi Professor, is class still running?'

Since beginning in my role as Assistant Professor in Human Rights and International Law, our campus has been regularly subjected to Israeli army incursions. Whereas the first term was relatively 'quiet', all things considered, during the 'Fall', the university is targeted almost daily, with property damaged, students injured, and classes disrupted. Tear gas produced by Combined Tactical Systems in Pennsylvania is fired by an Israeli Army heavily subsidised by the United States of America on a university campus part funded by USAID. The irony is not lost. Sound bombs, smoke grenades, and rubber-coated ball bearings—supposedly non-lethal tools for crowd dispersal—become a common feature of life on campus. The glass doors at the main entrance to the university have been smashed so many times that the decision has been taken to forgo having them replaced, at least for now. Alongside books, laptops, chargers, and other teaching essentials, I quickly learn the value in bringing an onion (or two) to work—sniffing a sliced onion being one of the best ways to ward off the impact of tear gas. The Palestinian Red Crescent, a humanitarian organisation linked to the International Red Cross, have permanently deployed an ambulance on site should any serious escalation require staff or students to receive expeditious medical treatment. Students have been arrested and bundled into the back of Israeli jeeps and several university staff have been threatened. Study abroad students from a number of Bard College affiliates have been evacuated as a result of the perceived threat to their safety and well-being, and the annual visit from Bard College staff in New York has been cancelled.

Shaking off the frustration of having to navigate the increasingly dangerous network of Israeli checkpoints that carve up the West Bank, those who make it to the class are engaged, prepared, and ready to debate and interrogate the rationale behind established legal norms. Against the omnipresent backdrop of attempted Zionist settler colonial erasure, including attacks on the delivery of a university level education, my colleagues and I, comprising a hybrid mix of international and local scholars, have managed to keep our classes running. Over the course of the semester, we have examined the theoretical underpinnings of *Jus Ad Bellum* and *Jus In Bello*, unpacked the origins of International Humanitarian Law, debated the legal issues behind the so-called global 'war on terror', argued the foundations behind the ever-expanding quasi-legal practice of transitional justice, and critiqued the role of the International Criminal Court.

But today feels different; the atmosphere in the room is subdued, and everything seems a little flat. Most of my students appear distracted and the quietness of the classroom jars with a commotion coming from outside in the communal plaza where a large group of students have gathered. Undeterred, I plough on and begin to introduce our topic: 'unpacking the role of truth commissions in transitional and post-conflict settings'. No-one bites. Sitting opposite me, one of my most engaged students, a young female from *Al Arroub* refugee camp, located on the outskirts of Hebron, looks visibly upset. I ask her, is everything ok? 'Professor' she replies, 'What is the point in talking about any of this? They killed my cousin Hasan last week. That noise you hear outside are his friends and family. He was a student here. Why are we wasting our time talking about any of this? There is no such thing as justice in Palestine'.

Hasan Albo was the third Palestinian student from Al Quds University, murdered during my time of employment, shot dead on the 13th November 2015 in the West Bank village of Halhul, 5 km from the Palestinian city of Hebron. At the beginning of the semester, 22nd September 2015, Diya Al-Talahmeh was murdered in the West Bank village of Khursa. And on the 3rd October 2015, Muhannad Halabi, a final year Law student from the village of Surda close to Ramallah, was shot dead in the Old City of Jerusalem whilst engaged in an attack on Israeli settlers that many consider to be the 'trigger' moment for the wider youth-led uprising. In the space of 3 months, my students lost three of their university peers, often in contentious circumstances. They experienced sustained attacks on their university, had their education disrupted daily, and were subjected to heightened levels of dehumanisation at the various checkpoints on their way to and from class. Facebook pages were transformed into online spaces of memorialisation and solidarity, adorned with the images of the many other young people from across the region who had been killed. Many students had been physically hurt as a result of the incursions on to the campus, others had been wounded during rioting that flared up in flashpoint areas closer to home, and nearly all of us, staff and students alike, were emotionally impacted, albeit with a vastly unequal exposure to risk. During this time, from the beginning of October some 260 Palestinians (including 57 minors) were killed by Israeli Occupation Forces, and many others injured. When it was impossible to make it to campus, my colleagues and I pivoted to online learning (long before the great Zoom awakening of 2020) to hold tutorials and discussion groups using a number of social media platforms. Despite what was unfolding, and the myriad challenges that they all had to overcome, every student in the class managed to successfully complete their course, to submit their work, finish assignments, and progress on to a new academic semester.

I left Al Quds University at the end of 2015 to take up a new position back home in Ireland, but the time I spent working with my students in Palestine remains the most formative of my academic career. The many hours we spent debating and critiquing the language and practice of transitional justice, challenging its Western liberal foundation and the manner in which it has enjoyed a burgeoning global appeal, has helped determine my arrival at this important personal and professional juncture. As I hope to show throughout the conversation that follows, in spaces blighted by sustained attempts at settler colonial erasure and met with subsequent anti-colonial resistance, the imposition of transitional justice interventions can be deflating, have a debilitating effect, and thus only ever provide a ruse of 'justice' whilst failing to meaningfully agitate for a reversal of the status quo. In this sense, transitional justice acts as a mode of containment, an extension of a peacebuilding model that has been so utterly damaging in terms of pursuing Palestinian liberation.

In Palestine, where the battle for existence remains as pronounced now as ever, our role as critical scholars must be to fundamentally evaluate and critique more fulsomely the role that transitional justice interventions being trialled, assume amidst the backdrop of an enduring, internationally sponsored, attempt at Zionist settler colonial erasure.

Whilst I wasn't able to adequately answer at the time, I hope my student knows that her line of questioning sparked in me a deeper and much-needed process of personal reflection, some of which has helped to shape the critique that follows. I am indebted to her and to all her colleagues in the class who were able to cut through the liberal fog and get right to the point.

Belfast, Ireland   Brendan Ciarán Browne

Acknowledgments

In reaching this important juncture in my academic career, I am lucky to have benefitted from the personal support and intellectual guidance of so many friends and comrades spanning cities, countries, and disciplines. In encouraging me to join him in Palestine in 2009 on a trip that has had an enduring impact on my personal and professional life ever since, I extend a special thanks to James Draper. During time spent at the Kenyon Institute in East Jerusalem (between 2010 and 2012), I am particularly grateful to Omar Shweiki, Mandy Turner, Saif Salah, Sami Salah, and Aengus Ó Dochartaigh, all of whom challenged me to think more critically about Palestine and who invested their time and energy in making that happen.

Whilst based at the Al Quds University (Bard College) Palestine (2015), I was fortunate to be surrounded by an incredible community of individuals, including colleagues who demonstrated unparalleled commitment to providing a first-class educational experience amidst the most challenging of circumstances. These remain persons who I hold in the highest regard, including Casey Asprooth-Jackson, Emilio Dabed, Emilio Distretti, Lucy Flamm, Elsa Raker, Yazid Albadarin, Yara Alafandi, and Munir Nuseibah. I am also grateful to the many others I met that year including Elian Weizmann, and to all my friends in Bethlehem who have helped make the place truly a second home, including: Odette, Tariq, Mazen, Mohammad, and Mike.

A special word of thanks is reserved for my good friend and comrade Maath Musleh who I met in 2015 and who has selflessly invested his time and energy into ensuring that I better understand Palestine and the struggle for liberation. To Bana Abu Zuluf for providing detailed comments and feedback on earlier drafts. Your critical eyes and commitment to 'calling it as it is' has helped sharpen the focus of this work. Thank you to Adler J Pruitt for providing much valued research assistance, and to my friend Elaine Bradley for many critical conversations we have had about Palestine over the years. In singling out my comrade and friend Mohsen al-Attar, I note the significance of his own work in helping shape my thinking on Palestine. As a scholar, comrade, and fellow agitator, his example is a source of guidance and inspiration, particularly when it comes to challenging me to speak with clarity of conviction. For that, and so much more, thank you.

To all the students I had the pleasure of working with and learning from in Palestine in 2015: Hanade, Mays, Shahd, Amera, Wiam, Aysha, Shireen, Jude, Shoroq, Bana, Lara, Aseel, Jawad, Hanaa, Shahd, Nada, Leena, Amanie, Nagham, Aida, Aya, Lina, Ola, Haneen, Ranin, Hala, and Batoul. I am forever indebted to you all for your searing insights in the classroom and for the support, encouragement, and warm welcome you gave me as an outsider in your space.

My community in Belfast provides the supportive platform upon which I feel empowered to continue in my work. As always, a special thank you to my family, Marie, Paul, Catherine, Maeve, and Niall and a note of gratitude to colleagues at Trinity College Dublin (Belfast Campus). A special thanks to the staff at the Guillemot Café, Ballyhackamore, who provided a space to read, write, and have the craic, all whilst keeping me topped up at all times.

Finally, to my wife Emma, for constantly challenging me to go further and for providing the encouragement and support required to keep pushing in any project. Your work in Palestine is a source of inspiration to me and it is the greatest of honours to be able to tread this path together. 'There is no tomorrow in yesterday, so let us advance'.

Contents

1 Introduction 1
2 Transitional Justice and Enforcing the 'Peace' on Palestine 23
3 Truth, Acknowledgement, and Combatting 'Memoricide' 41
4 Pursuing International Criminal Justice, the ICC, and Palestine 61
5 Conclusion 79

Index 95

CHAPTER 1

Introduction

Abstract Against the backdrop of ongoing attempted Zionist settler colonial erasure in historic Palestine and myriad failed international peacebuilding interventions, to what extent can transitional justice practices help shift the 'conflict' climate on the ground and in so doing, platform meaningful debates around 'justice' that are focused on meaningful decolonisation? In this scene setting chapter, the reader is provided an overview of the structure of the book. The focus of the various thematic chapters is introduced, including the weaponisation of peacebuilding in the context of Palestine, truth recovery and the role played by grassroots organisations in countering Israeli state-sponsored denial, and finally the role of 'top-down' International Criminal Justice interventions pursued by political elites (and more recently NGOs in Palestine). In addition, the reader is provided a note on terminology, highlighting that, despite the existence of a rich, theoretical grounding, there remains a blind spot, particularly amongst those invested in the language of transitional justice, to frame the Palestine-Israel 'conflict' in the language of settler colonialism, which in turn reduces the particulars when it comes to appraising relevant tools for bringing an end to or resolving the situation.

Keywords Transitional justice · Settler colonialism · Intervention · Peacebuilding

© The Author(s), under exclusive license to Springer Nature Switzerland AG 2023
B. C. Browne, *Transitional (in)Justice and Enforcing the Peace on Palestine*, Rethinking Peace and Conflict Studies, https://doi.org/10.1007/978-3-031-25394-2_1

Injustice on a sufficiently large scale is a stronger, freer, and more masterful thing than justice... and... it is the advantage of the stronger that is the just.

Plato, *The Republic* (Book I 344d)

INTRODUCTION

In an already swollen field of critical scholarly work, the case for adding another outside voice on issues relating to settler colonialism, peacebuilding, and justice (or lack thereof) in Palestine needs to be particularly strong. As a field of academic enquiry, transitional justice (TJ) continues to fascinate interdisciplinarians focused on better understanding the challenges faced by societies moving beyond conflict, and in more recent times, the intersection between TJ and settler colonialism has been brought more sharply into focus (Nagy, 2022; Park, 2015, 2020). Set against the backdrop of ongoing Zionist settler colonialism met by subsequent anti-colonial struggle (Turner, 2015), and as an area where TJ interventions are increasingly being trialled by a range of actors as a mode of peacebuilding, this convergence between TJ and settler colonialism has generated fertile terrain for more critical scholarly activity. This book seeks to spotlight some of the ways that TJ practices have crept into Palestine, and in so doing draw attention to its limitations when it comes to pursuing a 'justice'-oriented future, one that is based on the need for decolonisation. It does so by drawing attention to several issues, including: TJ as an extension of a flawed peacebuilding model in Palestine, platforming some of the limitations associated with pursuing International Criminal Justice (ICJ) before the International Criminal Court (ICC), and by spotlighting issues related to truth recovery and combatting memoricide. The conclusion reached is thus: TJ interventions taking place in Palestine, in many instances, mirror other flawed peacebuilding approaches and help to further delineate the terms of what is deemed acceptable when it comes to resolving the 'conflict' (a term used advisably, as discussed in more detail below). In allowing for cursory consideration of 'justice' matters in isolation, whilst failing to properly address the wider, structural issues, those that stem from ongoing Zionist settler colonial erasure mean that, far from being radical or revolutionary, these interventions (often internationally sponsored and/or donor led) amount to a transitional (in)justice, mimicking other flawed peacebuilding strategies, and therefore only serve to sharpen the asymmetrical power imbalance that characterises the status quo and further illuminate the distinction between colonised and coloniser.

In a recent critical analysis of the South Africa Truth and Reconciliation Commission (TRC), Ronald Suresh Roberts (2020) decries what he refers to as the 'colonisation' of the process by the 'new science' of TJ. Far from providing justice by addressing the systemic, root causes of apartheid, the parameters of what amounted to justice were deliberately constrained and for the most part, were established by an overwhelmingly white group of liberal interventionists, many of whom had connections to big-business, and who were part of a cohort with little interest in meaningful 'reconciliation', instead seeking ways of controlling the narrative around an inevitably difficult transition. In 'How Transitional Justice colonized South Africa's TRC', Roberts (2020: 1) argues:

> In line with its agenda of substantive social history, the ANC intended to establish a new Gramscian "common sense" of anti-colonialism and self-determination to drive anti-apartheid transformation. As part of its additional aim for an institutional intervention, the ANC sought to renovate the inherited technology of the colonial commission of inquiry itself… these aims were overturned through the superimposition of "transitional justice" within the workings of the TRC.

As a long-term anti-apartheid campaigner, critical legal scholar and co-author of one of the seminal texts on truth, reconciliation and justice in South Africa (Asmal et al., 1997), Roberts is more than qualified to offer up this stinging critique. Far from delivering the platform for a fundamental revaluation of the structural injustices that had become so deeply ingrained within apartheid South Africa and which had given rise to the African National Congress' (ANC) radical and revolutionary struggle for liberation, the TRC's remit and aims were coordinated by those with a liberal preference for 'justice' one that prioritised attempts at reconciliation, rather than reparatory justice encompassing a meaningful process of decolonisation and associated need for transformative structural reform in post-apartheid South Africa. Those involved in designing the process effectively choreographed 'truth' revelation so as to ensure it remained rooted within the parameters of a 'commission' of inquiry (Roberts, 2020), a by-product of colonial era management. The result being that the process was subject to control and oversight, allowing for lip-service to be paid to the victims and a false equivalency to be drawn between apartheid violence and anti-colonial resistance. Tokenistic gestures around forgiveness and reconciliation could therefore be promoted for political expediency, rather than embarking on a more meaningful 'liberatory, anti-colonial truth and reconciliation process' (Asmal et al., 1997). What thus emerged was an indeterminate engagement in a process of 'transition' rather than addressing the need for a fundamental and radical desire to bring about structural change.

Referring to the language and practice of this 'new science' of TJ as being 'paternalistic' and as having an 'impure political vision', Roberts (2020: 3) argues that in the case of South Africa, TJ operates as a liberal idea and a set of failed pretensions. Not that it matters, but Robert's criticism is far from an outlier and is shared by others who have scrutinised the process, including Claire Moon (2006). In her insights provided in *Narrating Political Reconciliation*, Moon draws attention to a 'corporate-liberal abduction' of the original aims of the South African TRC by a (predominantly white) body of TJ expertise. By virtue of the importation of a language and praxis of TJ from the West, one that had useful cheerleaders in the academy who were vocal in extolling its virtues in spaces of post-conflict transition, the TRC was subject to 'translation, misinterpretation' (Roberts, 2020: 8) to the extent that its original stated aims would no longer have any meaningful, long-term impact. For Roberts (2020), anti-apartheid activist Steve Biko's warning that 'blacks need occasion to speak up and whites need to learn to listen' was not being heeded. Simply put; the SATRC was 'colonized' by the imposition of TJ. Roberts' rebuke of the poster child of TJ, a widely lauded example of how to platform difficult truths pertaining to past injustices in the public sphere in order to help a society move forward, will be unpalatable for some, particularly those who are invested (literally and metaphorically) in the promotion of similar models of TJ intervention in other conflict and post-conflict sites. However, it is important that one engages in this form of political reflexivity when interrogating such 'conflict' spaces (Abdelnour & Abu Moghli, 2021). The growth of scholarly work that challenges the suitability of importing TJ interventions from one transitional and 'post-conflict' space into a vastly different one is a welcome turn, with an increasing number of critical voices challenging those who vehemently promote such (typically Western driven) interventions to reflect on their suitability and appropriateness (Jamar, 2019; Madlingozi, 2010). This critical turn, I suggest, is even more pressing when it comes to unpacking the potentially deleterious role that TJ interventions often assume as a mode of peacebuilding when pressed into service in spaces of ongoing settler colonialism. Spotlighting 'justice' issues in settler colonial contexts has, for the most part, largely been eschewed by TJ scholars and practitioners up until relatively recently, and as such, more is demanded from TJ (Balint et al., 2014) in this regard.

By considering some of the limitations in relation to: truth recovery processes and the role played by grassroots organisations in countering Israeli state-sponsored denial, 'top-down' International Criminal Justice interventions pursued by political elites (and more recently NGOs in Palestine), and the way that the language and practice of TJ has become subsumed within the mainstream Israeli academy, my aim here is to unsettle and challenge what I see as the burgeoning growth of a problematic TJ orthodoxy in Palestine. In doing so, I hope to demonstrate that, more often than not, such TJ interventions act as an extension of a peacebuilding approach that has repeatedly been shown to be so utterly destructive. If not linked to an overarching goal of realising a decolonised Palestine, one that platforms conversations around a 'transition' that centres the need for 'justice', TJ interventions run the risk of providing a smoke-screen for continued Israeli control and colonial management of the Palestinian population, aided and abetted by a simultaneously impotent and complicit international community.

A Note on Terminology

Before going any further, at this stage I want to draw attention to the importance of language when referencing the 'conflict' in Palestine/Israel, highlighting the fact that 'Mastery over language', as the inimitable Frantz Fanon (1963: 18) suggested, 'affords remarkable power'. In the present context, definitions and discourse denote the parameters on what is to be viewed as possible, as a reasonable 'solution' to a wrongly distorted, perceivably intractable situation. In mistakenly defining the relationship between coloniser and colonised through the language of 'conflict', the parameters of resolution have become more rigidly set. This particular framing—through the language of 'conflict'— allows for the imposition of a dual-protagonist narrative, one which fundamentally misrepresents the settler colonial reality on the ground, and in turn reduces Zionist settler sponsored violence to be akin to Palestinian resistance. Defining the violence experienced in Palestine in terms other than Zionist settler colonialism dismisses the lived reality of millions of Palestinians whose lives are dictated to by a military occupation or those who live in forced exile in many of the neighbouring countries of the Levant, in a state of semi-permanent limbo, denied their legal right to return. From those who live in villages across the West Bank, violently fragmented to such an extent that they have come to resemble the Bantustans of apartheid South Africa, fractured, and dislocated from each other whilst surrounded by illegal Israeli settlements, to those who live under a permanent state of siege, whose daily calorie intake is monitored by the Israeli occupation controlling the Gaza Strip, use of the word 'conflict' denotes a parity of esteem that belies reality. Anyone who has spent time in Palestine, and who has subsequently engaged in even the most basic and cursory analysis, will quickly discern that there exist no equal protagonists, no equal access to arms and resources, no equal access to the global hegemonic system of international relations, and therefore no fair and level playing field (Browne & Bradley, 2021).

Words routinely used to describe the situation in Palestine and Israel include intractable, unresolvable, or the particularly nefarious, complex. Native claims to the land are framed as 'contested' or 'disputed' in a distortion of historical accuracy. Palestine's history is one of violent colonial intervention (Browne & Bradley, 2021) encompassing periods of Ottoman rule, British imperialism, Zionist settler colonialism beginning with mass migration in the mid-1800s (persisting in the present day), and a process of ongoing neo-colonialism facilitated through the use of internationally sponsored liberal peacebuilding practices (Haddad, 2016; Tartir, 2015; Turner & Shweiki, 2014). The situation is therefore anything but 'complex'; rather, it is quite straightforward—an indigenous battle for survival versus an attempt at permanent erasure through ethnic cleansing in order to realise the nationalist aspirations of a settler community. The literature around theorising on Israeli settler colonialism is hardly new, with well-established scholarly contributions from: Zurayk (1956), Sayegh (1965), and Abdo and Yuval-Davis (1995), and more recently through the work of Wolfe (1999, 2006), Masalha (2012), Shlaim (2012), Lloyd (2012), and Hawari et al. (2019). Taken together, these critical interventions reaffirm that what has been mis-defined as 'conflict' should be considered through the lens of Zionist settler colonialism facilitated by a range of actors each with vested interests, including *inter alia*: the United States of America (US), the European Union (EU), the UN, the Israeli state, the PA, and the PLO.

In defining settler colonialism, Veracini (2013: 313) refers to the circumstances whereby 'colonizers come to stay and to establish new political orders for themselves'. Such a framing in the present context is hardly problematic when one considers that the very language of 'settler' and 'colony' is routinely employed by the Israeli state itself when referencing their ongoing presence in historic Palestine; the illegal outposts created in the West Bank, and East Jerusalem referred to as literal 'settlements'. The logic of settler colonialism, as Wolfe (2006) and Veracini (2013) have argued, involves control of land, with such control varying over time (Park, 2020: 263). Processes that embody a settler colonial logic are 'Elimination, expansion, exceptionalism, and denial' (Collins, 2011: 31; Wolfe, 1999, 2006). Indigenous land (in this case, Palestinian land) that is confiscated is then in need of being 'settled' by the 'settler' (Israeli) population, a process that is achieved through a variety of means, including: physical relocation, forcible transfer of the native population, destruction of the native population (through physical violence, genocide), forced assimilation into the settler society, active discrediting of native claims to the land, and the use of colonial violence that renders life on the land for indigenous populations, untenable (Vanden Boer, 2020: 22).

However, despite the existence of a rich, theoretical grounding, there remains a blind spot amongst many of those invested in the language of TJ, to frame the Palestine-Israel 'conflict' in the language of settler colonialism. Marginalising the language of settler colonialism reduces the particulars when it comes to appraising relevant tools for bringing an end to or resolving the situation. TJ interventionists who place emphasis on the 'conflict' discourse and who subsequently eschew the language of colonialism help to foster 'symmetrical responsibility' in terms of issues that need to be resolved. This in turn means that an orthodoxy is generated whereby 'contested claims, contested narratives, contested accounts of events' are maintained and 'each party and their claim is accorded a validity' (Bradley, 2020). This 'dual-protagonist' thesis therefore reinforces and places limits around what amounts to 'justice'. Such a framing, yet again, demands Palestinian concession rather than meaningfully righting historical and present-day wrongs. The onus is placed squarely on the oppressed to display 'good will' to appease and mitigate the nationalist desires of the oppressor. Given that discourse and power are intimately linked (Said, 1984), nomenclature matters, as this book, and its use of language, seeks to demonstrate.

The book builds on previous published work which critiqued the suitability of such TJ interventions, including a foundational article I published in 2021, entitled: 'Disrupting Settler-Colonialism or Enforcing the Liberal 'Peace'? Transitional (In)Justice in Palestine-Israel'. In the article, I argued that any TJ praxis that fails to engage with meaningful conversations around decolonisation had the potential to amount to the dilution and individualisation of 'justice', whilst failing to address the root causes of the 'conflict' that centre on Zionism's ongoing settler colonial mission in historic Palestine. Rather than calling for a complete withdrawal from engaging in TJ practices in Palestine, I considered what steps, if any, could be taken to ensure a radicalisation of the process, asking for those who champion TJ in this context to eschew Western-led interventions in favour of solely Palestinian-led processes. Building on this piece, in this book I reinforce the call for a disruption to the liberal interpretation of TJ and argue that any TJ intervention that takes place must ensure that 'justice' issues in Palestine are considered solely through a decolonial lens. Despite being one of the most heavily analysed and researched geopolitical 'conflicts, there is a relative dearth of mainstream engagement with TJ in Palestine-Israel, a situation that Khoury (2021: 153) notes as strange given that 'it (transitional justice) touches upon crucial aspects to ending the conflict, such as dealing with historical injustices, decolonization, and the proposed one-state and two state solutions'. One of the earliest scholarly contributions to consider TJ in the context of Palestine-Israel was offered by Cohen (1995) in his text entitled *Justice in Transition? Prospects for a Palestinian-Israeli Truth Commission*. The article discussed whether TJ mechanisms linked to truth recovery, similar to the South African model discussed above, might offer the opportunity to draw a line under the past and therefore help to embed the purported gains of Oslo at a time when optimism for the infant 'Peace Process' remained relatively high. Since then, a growing corpus of scholarly work has developed, including articles by, *inter alia*: Peled and Rouhana (2004), Dudai (2007, 2010, 2013), Khoury (2016, 2021), Browne (2017, 2021), Jamar (2019), Dudai and Cohen (2020), and most recently Bracka (2021). Important single-issue analyses on memorialisation, commemoration, and truth recovery have been offered by others, including Broadhead (2020), Lentin (2013), Masalha (2012, 2015), and Nets-Zehngut (2012). Alongside academic analyses, local and international NGOs have embraced the language and practice of TJ, including several high-profile organisations such as the

Israeli-led *Zochrot* and the Bethlehem-based *BADIL*. TJ praxis can also be deduced in the work of other Palestinian NGOs, for example *Grassroots Al Quds* an organisation whose work aims at safeguarding Palestinian culture and heritage in Jerusalem at a time when such a presence remains under constant threat of erasure. Therefore, despite being relatively under critiqued, the language and praxis of TJ in Palestine-Israel is somewhat hidden in plain sight with TJ interventions being considered by a range of actors, including academics, international and local NGOs, and political elites. Many of the constituent elements that comprise TJ including truth recovery, criminal justice, memorialisation/commemoration, reparations, and institutional reform have, in some shape or form, been considered at various times, driven primarily by those committed to this form of peacebuilding, in an effort to conceive of 'reconciliation' in a 'conflict' viewed as intractable (Rouhana, 2018). However, the extent to which these have ensured meaningful progress towards a decolonial future in Palestine is open to debate.

'The global importance of Palestine', as Collins (2011: 1) has suggested, 'seems to be increasing in inverse proportion to the amount of territory controlled by Palestinians'. Indeed, reflecting on the impact of former United States President, Donald Trump's recent disastrous foray into what is most commonly (and inappropriately) referred to as the 'Middle East Peace Process', Toufic Haddad (2019) argued that Zionism's ongoing and expanding settler colonial mission, as supported almost universally by the West, has rendered Palestine 'on a precipice'. The slow and steady process of Zionist colonisation in historic Palestine, a stretch of land that runs from the Mediterranean Sea in the West to the Jordan River in the East, shows little sign of abating. The expansion of illegal settlements, the continued implementation of siege warfare enacted against Palestinian civilians in the Gaza Strip, the suppression of free speech and public dissent that criticises Israeli policies (recently evidenced through the criminalisation of leading human rights NGOs across the West Bank and Israel), the embedding of the infrastructure of apartheid that discriminates against Palestinians living in the (as yet undetermined) borders of Israel, and the criminalisation of Palestinian heritage and culture in the city of Jerusalem, all follow the same logic of settler colonial erasure 'in action' (Collins, 2011; Lloyd, 2012; Veracini, 2013, 2014). The international community have adopted a Janus-faced approach to 'conflict resolution', investing time, monies, and diplomatic energy into sponsorship of a 'two-state solution' by vigorously maintaining the promotion of a 'Peace Process' that has long since died, akin to rearranging deck chairs on the Titanic. Simultaneously, they have eschewed their responsibility as sovereign nation states to hold their rogue counterpart to account for multiple, flagrant breaches of international law. It is into this deeply asymmetrical 'conflict' space, characterised as settler colonial in nature that the mechanics and liberal promise of TJ have sought to take root, acting in much the same way as an extension of a peacebuilding approach that has been widely discredited by a rich and diverse body of scholarly critique (Haddad, 2016; Turner, 2012, 2015; Turner & Shweiki, 2014). Such interventions, I posit, operate so as to ensure that the privileged position of settler sovereignty is maintained and the decolonial aspirations of the colonised cast aside.

Akin to the critique of the South African TRC offered above by Roberts (2020),peacebuilding interventions linked to the 'new science' of TJ that fail to offer a decolonial means of addressing the structural issues and root causes of the 'conflict' in Palestine/Israel and which avoid the hard conversations around what a decolonial future in Palestine looks like, one that includes reparations (however conceived), act as a means of extension of the settler colonial paradigm that seeks to manage and erode legitimate expectations, and thus become part of the problem. TJ interventions that promote truth recovery, commemoration, memorialisation, or limited criminal justice whilst simultaneously failing to link the rationale underpinning Palestinian narratives of loss, dispossession, and historical injustice as being the result of ongoing Zionist principles that underpin the logic of settler colonialism, ethnic cleansing, and associated war crimes (more woolly mammoth than elephant in the room at this stage) serve the useful liberal function of providing lip-service whilst failing to rock the apple-cart, allowing for a continuous sense of 'transition' and a further marginalisation of issues relating to 'justice'. In much the same way, the pursuit of retributive justice, specifically through the outworking of the International Criminal Court or the International Court of Justice (the supreme examples of top-down TJ), helps to individualise and dislocate the 'justice'-related issues, resulting in a dilution of the much-needed joined-up and cohesive strategic thinking around structural asymmetries that require decolonisation. This 'justice for some', to borrow from Erakat (2019), can further become a useful tool that can be pressed into service of the coloniser in that it has the potential to sharpen the edges of Palestinian anti-colonial resistance, placing it alongside Israeli state-sponsored violence, marginalising the Palestinian cause in the court of public opinion.

On a surface level, promoting critical thinking around memorialisation, reparatory justice, commemoration, and inter-group dialogue may appear innovative and useful in shifting the 'conflict' climate on the ground. Such a claim is often advanced when the work in question involves conversations around TJ that take place in the bosom of the Israeli academy and are led by Israeli academics and their international allies. However, as I later argue, similar to the role played by the 'commission' of enquiry and Robert's (2020) critique of the South African TRC above, when such TJ conversations are rooted in, and led by institutions that benefit from their position as being emanations of the colonial power, the potential for meaningful 'justice' for Palestine, one that is truly decolonial, dissipates through the careful control and manipulation of the TJ narrative. Conversations around reconciliation can quickly be reduced to calls for collective amnesia, the right of return can be dismissed as whimsical sentiment, and reparations can be discussed in such a way as to ensure indigenous concession rather than settler compensation. The TJ that is subsequently promoted operates as a fig-leaf allowing for cursory consideration of issues in relative isolation and without due consideration to the broader structural concerns that lie at the heart of Zionism's ongoing settler colonial mission in historic Palestine. There is thus an allusion of 'doing something', of promoting a 'justice' that is based on mutual recognition of suffering, across all sides, which in turn serves to flatten the deep asymmetry that lies at the heart of the 'conflict'. More pressingly, by delineating the parameters around what amounts to 'justice' in such contexts, an orthodox position is established, one that can be difficult to dislodge, and which can subsequently marginalise other counter-narratives and legitimate forms of resistance. If it is to 'advance demands for decolonisation and be an ally to activities and movements that work towards that end' (Park, 2015: 273), TJ in the case of Palestine needs a radicalisation, a process that will require the hard conversations around decolonisation and an end to the settler colonial reality on the ground (Rouhana, 2018).

Transitional Justice to What End?

As has been noted by Nadim Khoury (2021) when it comes to appraising the role of TJ in the context of Palestine-Israel, it is important to ask two straightforward, but prescient questions, namely: 'Whose justice? [and] Which transition?'. Across Palestinian society, discerning agreement on what amounts to 'transition' itself has been subject to intra-factional, intra-familial, and geographic contestation. This is understandable when one considers that the day-to-day Palestinian experience of Zionist settler colonialism, whilst always violent, differs depending on a variety of factors, including: geographical location, socio economic, and political status. Palestinians living in East Jerusalem under threat of being evicted from their homes interact with the Israeli occupation in a way that differs from Palestinian residents being targeted across other urban spaces in the West Bank, such as Ramallah, Bethlehem, Jenin, and Nablus. Palestinians living in the Gaza Strip experience the scourge of barbaric siege warfare alongside having to deal with the constant fear of Israeli bombing campaigns that have culminated in 4 wars in 13 years. The Palestinian Bedouin communities, those who live at the sharp edge of the Israeli occupation, experience daily battles that threaten their agrarian livelihood. Those who live as Palestinian citizens of Israel experience discrimination and social exclusion under an apartheid regime. And those who live across the wider Palestinian diaspora, including the many millions of Palestinian refugees living in Lebanon, Syria, and Jordan, experience the same loss and yearning for a return home. However, despite the common thread being a violent encounter with, and resistance to Zionist settler colonialism, discerning a shared and cohesive acceptance of the best way to achieve a decolonial future has not always been easy. As such, in Palestine, there exists an almost 'ambivalent and often confusing post-Oslo political condition' one that oscillates 'between the anticolonial and the postcolonial' (Sen, 2020: 37). It is into this somewhat hotly contested space that TJ's most fervent supporters have sought to intervene.

Those who are invested (literally) in the notion of Palestinian statehood include many of whom have benefitted from the establishment of the Palestinian Authority (PA), Palestinian capitalists who have returned from abroad with the aim of investing in a 'new' State of Palestine (Dana, 2020; Rabie, 2021). Historically, amongst many in this group, there has been a willingness to accept a 'transition' towards a process of 'post-conflict' that is broadly speaking 'statist' and which involves: an end to Israeli occupation of the West Bank, an end to the siege of Gaza, implementation of a two-state reality (with links between the Gaza Strip and the West Bank), final state borders that match the 1967 armistice line, and an acceptance of East Jerusalem as the capital city of Palestine. Such a resolution and successful 'transition' would therefore inevitably involve a softening of long-held 'red-lines' including the full implementation of the right of return for Palestinian refugees, despite public recommitments to the contrary (Browne, 2013). For others, 'transition' that does not include the full process of de-zionification and a commitment to the decolonisation of historic Palestine, a process which Barghouti (2011: 165) has noted is, on the one hand, 'the only logical, legal and moral reparation for the native population' would be incomplete. Ensuring a steadfast commitment to implementing the right of return for all Palestinian refugees is simply non-negotiable.

For many scholars interested in applying TJ in and for Palestine, there is a belief that in considering certain high-profile 'justice' issues whilst the 'conflict' is ongoing, the potential exists to produce a more conciliatory political climate, which in turn can allow for meaningful 'peacebuilding' practices to be implemented. In 'recasting the former in light of the latter - i.e., by attempting to fit the Israeli-Palestinian conflict into the transitional paradigm' (Meyerstein, 2006: 282/283), it is suggested that any potential stumbling blocks in the future 'will reveal themselves and challenges seen elsewhere will appear more pronounced'. Building on this proposition, the reader is asked to consider the following questions as you work your way through the chapters: firstly, against the backdrop of Zionist attempts at settler colonial erasure in historic Palestine, to what extent do TJ interventions help shift 'on-the-ground' realities? Secondly, how has the language and praxis of TJ been adopted by a range of actors in Palestine, including international non-governmental organisations, local Palestinian and Israeli non-governmental organisations, and the academic community? Thirdly, is the pursuit of International Criminal Justice and truth recovery useful in helping to platform meaningful conversation about ending and reversing Zionist settler colonial practice in Palestine? Can a TJ approach aid in facilitating the much needed conversations around decolonisation or are they an example of a 'new science' operating as a set of flawed peacebuilding interventions?

In her recent work which focuses on TJ taking place in spaces characterised as settler colonial in nature, A. S. J. Park (2020, 2022) has called for a 'radicalisation' of the field in order to ensure the recentring of Indigenous voices when considering residual justice issues in settled, settler democracies. Through reference to the need to recognise the harm experienced by indigenous communities in Canada, Park (2020: 277) argues:

In order to theorise a decolonising TJ, we must train our gaze on a critical encounter within settler colonialism. Settler colonialism should not be understood as an autonomous actor, but as a project that is enacted and sustained by *settlers* and the ongoing fact, discourses and practices of *settlement*.

In building on Park's insights, it follows that in spaces characterised by ongoing settler colonialism, the role that TJ interventions must assume if they are to be truly invested in native justice is to spotlight the true nature of the coloniser's relationship with the Indigenous community, and in so doing disrupt, agitate, challenge, and ultimately act as an ally to decolonisation. TJ practices that fail to do so run the risk of serving the rather nefarious purpose of maintaining the hegemonic position of the coloniser at the expense of the colonised by promoting soft 'justice' efforts in isolation and detached from the broader decolonial struggle. In the case of Palestine, meaningful radicalisation will demand the continuous centring of the legitimate demand for decolonisation, at every opportunity. Failure to do so will mean that TJ continues to act as an extension of peacebuilding interventions that have been enforced upon Palestine and the Palestinians, which have been deeply flawed and which have failed to act as an ally in helping to halt or reverse Zionism's ongoing attempt at Palestinian erasure. In drawing attention to the similarities between TJ interventions and peacebuilding practices (broadly defined) in Palestine, I am not seeking to re-invent the wheel. A rich and growing body of scholarly work has done much by way of heavy lifting (Balint et al., 2014; Sriram, 2007). However, it is hoped that by critiquing the examples provided in this book and by encouraging others to appreciate the limitations and potentialities for reform, I can continue the conversation that challenges others to consider more meaningfully the impact of their involvement in such work. Given that Palestine remains an area of ongoing anti-colonial struggle (Turner, 2015), the need to platform these conversations around TJ interventions that take place in the region is, I suggest, more urgent and pressing than ever.

A Process of Maturation

In his paper 'On transitional justice and the production of victims' (2010) leading South African scholar and activist, Tshepo Madlingozi challenges those involved in TJ work to engage in a greater process of reflection.

Critiquing the emergence of what he defines as a TJ industry, and in citing Alcoff (1991: 7) Madlingozi (2010: 210) asks, 'Is the discursive practice of speaking for others ever a legitimate practice and if so, what is the criterion for its validity? In particular, is it ever valid to speak for others who are unlike me, or who are less privileged than me?' Reflecting more specifically on the 'transitional justice entrepreneur' (2010: 211), Madlingozi draws attention to the role that TJ interventionists play in defining and categorising victims, speaking on their behalf, packaging their experience in a digestible way, in order to sell their victimhood on the international stage. This stinging critique should cause discomfort for all involved in TJ, particularly those in the West who choose to conduct research overseas in areas where conflict and violence have been the norm. For decades, Palestine and the Palestinians have been the subject of international categorisation, with their experience of victimhood, trauma, and loss curated by academics, an issue that Edward Said (1984) so eruditely highlighted in his famous treatise 'permission to narrate'. As former UN Special Rapporteur for Palestine (2008–2014) and Professor Emeritus of International Law, Richard Falk has noted:

> Part of the Palestinian tragedy, ever since the fall of the Ottoman Empire, is that others have again and again presumed to talk on behalf of the Palestinian people. Because of the manner in which the world is organized, these alien voices have consistently overridden Palestinian voices on the basis of geopolitical calculations and Orientalist thinking, to the detriment of the Palestinian people.

Heeding Madlingozi's (2010) warning is an important anchoring point for my thinking in this book, and like all scholarly work, my contribution here is based on a process of personal maturation in terms of critical thinking on Palestine. Allow me to elaborate. In autumn 2015, I wrote a book chapter which was eventually published in the *Research Handbook of Transitional Justice* entitled 'Transitional Justice and the case of Palestine' (Browne, 2017). In the chapter, I put forward ideas and views on TJs application in the region that in hindsight, were underdeveloped and 'safe' in terms of language used and recommendations made, heavily edited to such an extent that it lost the much needed critical edge. The chapter fell afoul of what Rouhana (2018: 654) lucidly refers to as a 'psychologising' of the 'conflict', obscuring the 'true nature: the power structures, the hierarchies of dominance, the politics of ethnic privileging, and the guiding political and ideological outlooks of each group'. My understanding and thinking around conflict, peacebuilding, and 'justice' have thankfully evolved, based on my experience working in and on Palestine, including time spent with critical colleagues, students, and activists in the Palestinian university sector. The ceaseless energy of Palestinian scholars has ensured that production of a corpus of critical Palestinian work, particularly that which has a transnational appeal, is never ending, all of which has had a profound influence on how I have come to better appreciate TJ's limitations when practised in the region. An ever-expanding body of work from the sub-discipline of 'Third World Approaches to International Law' (TWAIL) has been particularly useful in helping me to gain a more nuanced appreciation for TJs liberal underpinnings, most notably, important works from: Mutua (2000), Mutua and Anghie (2000) and many other contributions including Natarajan et al. (2016), Reynolds and Xavier (2016), Gathii (2018), and Al Attar (2020). Therefore, far from proposing any unhelpful and unwarranted solutions to the 'conflict', my aim here is to shine a light on what I view as some of the problematics pertaining to TJ intervention in the region.

Overview

Beginning first by charting the development of the sub-discipline of TJ, I note its liberal origins and highlight the various salient approaches that have generated a TJ orthodoxy. The reader is introduced to the core principles of TJ, including: truth recovery, reparations, institutional reform, and criminal prosecution. In so doing, I seek to highlight that the practices that have come to define TJ remain very much situated firmly within the values of other forms of peacebuilding intervention, many of which are Eurocentric in their outlook and aims. The convergence of TJ and liberal peacebuilding is highlighted alongside the work of others who have spotlighted some of the limitations of the sub-discipline. I next turn to chronicle the deeply flawed process of enforcing 'peace' on Palestine, spotlighting the various ways in which the international community have been involved in maintaining a deeply inequitable status quo, through reference to leading scholarly work, before moving on to considering issues relating to grassroots attempts at combating Israeli state-sponsored denial and obfuscation of the truth surrounding the foundational violence that lies at the heart of the Zionist state-building project. With specific reference to the work of Zochrot, I unpack what I (and others) have outlined as being some of the limitations with this form of truth recovery process, including issues relating to who has 'permission to narrate' such truths of the past. Next, I turn to consider the top-down, elite-driven move towards embracing International Criminal Justice, particularly the recent engagement with the International Criminal Court (ICC). In so doing, I draw on a rich body of Palestinian and international legal scholarship that has sought to highlight the weaknesses and potentialities around such strategies. In concluding, I note how TJ has been subsumed within the apparatus of the Israeli academy, the supposed last bastion of Israeli liberalism, and invite greater reflection on some of the challenges that this recent turn presents. I ask what a radicalisation of TJ in this context may look like, and call on those committed to TJ in the region to platform conversations that centre on the need for decolonial reparations with a specific focus on future 'repair' in Palestine being one area for potential, meaningful TJ engagement.

My aim throughout is not to provide definitive answers, TJ has always operated in the grey spaces and has benefitted from rigorous disagreement and divergent viewpoints. However, so too has TJ benefitted from the promotion of certain ideologies and voices at the expense of others. In sparking a debate pertaining to TJs deflating impact when pressed into service in spaces of ongoing settler colonial erasure, I am challenging those who are engaged in such work to hit pause and reflect more critically on whether their promotion of such work is less about alleviating the suffering of others and more to do with an avoidance of addressing the settler colonial elephant in the room.

References

Abdelnour, S., & Abu Moghli, M. (2021). Researching violent contexts: A call for political reflexivity. *Organization*. https://doi.org/10.1177/13505084211030646

Abdo, N., & Yuval-Davis, N. (1995). Palestine, Israel and the Zionist settler project. *Unsettling Settler Societies: Articulations of Gender, Race Ethnicity and Class, 11*, 291.

Al Attar, M. (2020). TWAIL: A paradox within a paradox. *International Community Law Review, 22*(2), 163–196. https://doi.org/10.1163/18719732-12341426

Alcoff, L. (1991). The problem of speaking for others. *Cultural Critique*, (20), 5–32.

Asmal, K., Asmal, L., & Roberts, R. S. (1997). *Reconciliation through truth: A reckoning of apartheid's criminal governance*. New Africa Books.

Balint, J., Evans, J., & McMillan, N. (2014). Rethinking transitional justice, redressing indigenous harm: A new conceptual approach. *International Journal of Transitional Justice*, 8(2), 194–216. https://doi.org/10.1093/ijtj/iju004

Barghouti, O. (2011). *BDS: Boycott, divestment, sanctions: The global struggle for Palestinian rights*. Haymarket Books.

Bracka, J. (2021). *Transitional Justice for Israel/Palestine*. Springer International Publishing.

Bradley, E. (2020). Conflict or colonialism? Discover Society. https://discoversociety.org/2020/10/07/on-the-front-line-conflict-vs-colonialism-in-palestine/

Broadhead, L. A. (2020). Scales of justice: putting remembrance back on the map in Palestine and Mi'kma'ki. *Settler Colonial Studies*, 10(3), 331–352.

Browne, B. (2013). Commemoration in conflict. *Journal of Comparative Research in Anthropology and Sociology*, 4(02), 143–163.

Browne, B. C. (2017). Transitional justice and the case of Palestine. In *Research handbook on transitional justice* [Preprint]. https://www.elgaronline.com/view/edcoll/9781781955307/9781781955307.00034.xml

Browne, B. C. (2021). Disrupting settler-colonialism or enforcing the liberal "peace"? Transitional (in)justice in Palestine-Israel. *Journal of Holy Land and Palestine Studies*, 20(1), 1–27. https://doi.org/10.3366/hlps.2021.0255

Browne, B. C., & Bradley, E. (2021). Promoting Northern Ireland's peace-building experience in Palestine–Israel: Normalising the status quo. *Third World Quarterly*, 1–19. https://doi.org/10.1080/01436597.2021.1903310

Cohen, S. (1995). Justice in transition? Prospects for a Palestinian-Israeli truth commission. *Middle East Report* (194/195), 2–5.

Collins, J. (2011). *Global palestine*. Hurst Publishers.

Dana, T. (2020). Crony capitalism in the Palestinian authority: A deal among friends. *Third World Quarterly*, 41(2), 247–263.

Dudai, R. (2007). A model for dealing with the past in the Israeli Palestinian context. *International Journal of Transitional Justice*, 1(2), 249–267. https://doi.org/10.1093/ijtj/ijm019

Dudai, R., & Cohen, H. (2010). Dealing with the past when the conflict is still present. In *Localizing transitional justice* (pp. 228–252). Stanford University Press.

Dudai, R. (2013). Does any of this matter? Transitional justice and the Israeli–Palestinian conflict. In *Crime, social control and human rights* (pp. 367–380). Willan.

Dudai, R., & Cohen, H. (2020). Dealing with the past when the conflict is still present. In *Localizing transitional justice* (Chapter 11, pp. 228–252).

Stanford University Press. https://www.degruyter.com/document/doi/10.1515/9780804774635-014/html (Accessed: 4 August 2021).
Erakat, N. (2019). *Justice for some: Law and the question of Palestine*. Stanford University Press.
Fanon, F. (1963). *The wretched of the earth* (R. Philcox, Trans., 239 pp.). Grove, 2004.
Gathii, J. T. (2018). The agenda of Third World Approaches to International Law (TWAIL). In *International legal theory: Foundations and frontiers*. Cambridge University Press.
Haddad, T. (2016). *Palestine Ltd.: Neoliberalism and nationalism in the occupied territory*. Bloomsbury.
Haddad, T. (2019). Palestine on a precipice. *New Politics* (Accessed: 10 October 2022). https://newpol.org/issue_post/palestineon-a-precipice
Hawari, Y., Plonski, S., & Weizman, E. (2019). Seeing Israel through Palestine: Knowledge production as anti-colonial praxis. *Settler Colonial Studies, 9*(1), 155–175. https://doi-org.elib.tcd.ie/10.1080/2201473X.2018.1487129, https://doi.org/10.1080/2201473X.2018.1487129
Jamar, A. (2019). The crusade of transitional justice tracing the journeys of hegemonic claims. In The British Academy (Ed.), *Violence and democracy. UK-India early career knowledge symposium on violence and democracy* (pp. 53–59). British Academy. https://www.thebritishacademy.ac.uk/publications/knowledge-frontiers-violence-and-democracy (Accessed: 14 July 2021).
Khoury, N. (2016). National narratives and the Oslo peace process: How peacebuilding paradigms address conflicts over history. *Nations and Nationalism, 22*(3), 465–483. https://doi.org/10.1111/nana.12166
Khoury, N. (2021). Transitional justice in Palestine/Israel: Whose justice? Which transition? In L. Farsakh (Ed.), *Rethinking statehood in Palestine*. University of California Press. https://doi.org/10.1525/luminos.113.g
Lentin, R. (2013). *Co-memory and melancholia: Israelis memorialising the Palestinian Nakba*. Co-memory and melancholia, 1–212.
Lloyd, D. (2012). Settler colonialism and the state of exception: The example of Palestine/Israel. *Settler Colonial Studies, 2*(1), 59–80. https://doi.org/10.1080/2201473X.2012.10648826
Madlingozi, T. (2010). On transitional justice entrepreneurs and the production of victims. *Journal of Human Rights Practice, 2*(2), 208–228.
Masalha, N. (2012). *The Palestine Nakba: Decolonising history, narrating the subaltern, reclaiming memory*. Zed Books.
Masalha, N. (2015). Settler-colonialism, memoricide and indigenous toponymic memory: The appropriation of Palestinian place names by the Israeli state. *Journal of Holy Land and Palestine Studies, 14*(1), 3–57.

Meyerstein, A. (2006). Transitional justice and post-conflict Israel/Palestine: Assessing the applicability of the truth commission paradigm. *Case Western Reserve Journal of International Law, 38*, 281.

Moon, C. (2006). Narrating political reconciliation: Truth and reconciliation in South Africa. *Social & Legal Studies, 15*(2), 257–275. https://doi.org/10.1177/0964663906063582

Mutua, M. (2000). What is TWAIL? *Proceedings of the ASIL Annual Meeting, 94*, 31–38.

Mutua, M., & Anghie, A. (2000). What is TWAIL? *Proceedings of the Annual Meeting (American Society of International Law), 94*, 31–40.

Nagy, R. (2022). Transformative justice in a settler colonial transition: Implementing the UN declaration on the rights of indigenous peoples in Canada. *The International Journal of Human Rights, 26*(2), 191–216.

Natarajan, U., et al. (2016). Introduction: TWAIL—On praxis and the intellectual. *Third World Quarterly, 37*(11), 1946–1956. https://doi.org/10.1080/01436597.2016.1209971

Nets-Zehngut, R. (2012). Israeli memory of the Palestinian refugee problem. *Peace Review, 24*(2), 187–194.

Park, A. S. J. (2015). Settler colonialism and the politics of grief: Theorising a decolonising transitional justice for Indian residential schools. *Human Rights Review, 16*(3), 273–293. https://doi.org/10.1007/s12142-015-0372-4

Park, A. S. J. (2020). Settler colonialism, decolonization and radicalizing transitional justice. *International Journal of Transitional Justice, 14*(2), 260–279. https://doi.org/10.1093/ijtj/ijaa006

Park, A. S. (2022). Settler colonialism and the South African TRC: Ambivalent denial and democratisation without decolonisation. *Social & Legal Studies, 31*(2), 216–237.

Peled, Y., & Rouhana, N. N. (2004). Transitional justice and the right of return of the Palestinian refugees: Theoretical perspectives. *Theoretical Inquiries in Law, 5*(2), 317–332.

Reynolds, J., & Xavier, S. (2016). "The dark corners of the world": TWAIL and International Criminal Justice. *Journal of International Criminal Justice*. https://doi.org/10.1093/jicj/mqw053

Roberts, R. S. (2020). How 'transitional justice' colonized SouthAfrica's TRC. *Modern Languages Open, 34*(1), 1–15.

Rouhana, N. N. (2018). Decolonization as reconciliation: Rethinking the national conflict paradigm in the Israeli-Palestinian conflict. *Ethnic and Racial Studies, 41*(4), 643–662. https://doi.org/10.1080/01419870.2017.1324999

Said, E. (1984). Permission to narrate. *Journal of Palestine Studies, 13*(3), 27–48. https://doi.org/10.2307/2536688

Sayegh, F. A. (1965). *Zionist colonialism in Palestine* (Vol. 1). Research Center, Palestine Liberation Organization.
Sen, S. (2020). *Decolonizing Palestine: Hamas between the anticolonial and the postcolonial*. Cornell University Press.
Shlaim, A. (2012). The iron wall revisited. *Journal of Palestine Studies, 41*(2), 80–98. https://doi.org/10.1525/jps.2012.XLI.2.80
Sriram, C. L. (2007). Justice as peace? Liberal peacebuilding and strategies of transitional justice. *Global Society, 21*(4), 579–591.
Rabie, K. (2021). *Palestine is throwing a party and the whole world is invited: Capital and state building in the West Bank*. Duke University Press.
Tartir, A. (2015). Securitised development and Palestinian authoritarianism under Fayyadism. *Conflict, Security & Development, 15*(5), 479–502.
Turner, M. (2012). Completing the circle: Peacebuilding as colonial practice in the occupied Palestinian territory. *International Peacekeeping, 19*(4), 492–507. https://doi.org/10.1080/13533312.2012.709774
Turner, M. (2015). Peacebuilding as counterinsurgency in the occupied Palestinian territory. *Review of International Studies, 41*(1), 73–98. https://doi.org/10.1017/S0260210514000072
Turner, M., & Shweiki, O. (2014). *Decolonizing Palestinian political economy: De-development and beyond*. Springer.
Vanden Boer, D. (2020). *Touristic entanglements: Settler colonialism, worldmaking and the politics of tourism in Palestine* (Doctoral dissertation). Ghent University.
Veracini, L. (2013). The other shift: Settler colonialism, Israel, and the occupation. *Journal of Palestine Studies, 42*(2), 26–42. https://doi.org/10.1525/jps.2013.42.2.26
Veracini, L. (2014). Understanding colonialism and settler colonialism as distinct formations. *Interventions, 16*(5), 615–633. https://doi.org/10.1080/1369801X.2013.858983
Wolfe, P. (1999). *Settler colonialism*. A&C Black.
Wolfe, P. (2006). Settler colonialism and the elimination of the native. *Journal of Genocide Research, 8*(4), 387–409.
Zurayk, C. (1956). *The meaning of disaster*. Khayat.

CHAPTER 2

Transitional Justice and Enforcing the 'Peace' on Palestine

Abstract In this chapter, I highlight core transitional justice principles with a view to noting the various components that have come to represent a transitional justice orthodoxy. The convergence between TJ and peacebuilding has evolved to such an extent that the two have become almost synonymous, sharing much in terms of liberal, Eurocentric ideology, and enjoying the benefits that accompany becoming mainstreamed within the operational policies of the UN. In unpacking the ways that peacebuilding has been weaponised against the Palestinians, thus stifling the pursuit of a justice-oriented, decolonial reality, I note how, when pressed into service in areas of ongoing settler colonial violence, TJ interventions can have a deflating effect, particularly when they fail to properly platform the legitimate decolonial demands of an Indigenous community battling against attempts at their permanent erasure.

Keywords Transitional justice · Liberal peacebuilding · International intervention · Oslo accords

> They steal your bread then give you a crumb of it… then they demand you thank them for their generosity… O their audacity.
>
> Ghassan Kanafani

© The Author(s), under exclusive license to Springer Nature Switzerland AG 2023
B. C. Browne, *Transitional (in)Justice and Enforcing the Peace on Palestine*, Rethinking Peace and Conflict Studies,
https://doi.org/10.1007/978-3-031-25394-2_2

Introduction

Since its emergence as a sub-discipline in its own right, TJ has been the object of much by way of academic scrutiny, with its intrinsic interdisciplinarity ensuring that the net of intellectual interest has been cast far and wide. Academic journals, research centres, and university degree programmes, to name but a few, have helped to foster the growth of, what some have referred to as a TJ 'industry', established in harmony alongside myriad NGOs and think tanks. According to Baker and Obradovic-Wochnik (2016: 282/283) 'Peacebuilding and transitional justice, like any other analytical concepts, exist because institutions and scholars have constructed them as objects that can be known about... Both are analytical categories imposed on the complexity of post-conflict societies and interventions, socially constructed through labelling and citation'. Across the globe, in areas characterised as being in a period of 'post-conflict' transition, the language and praxis of TJ has become common parlance and deeply embedded within the fabric of emergent, fledgling states, those who have been encouraged to consider an array of residual issues linked to the past, in order to help safeguard the benefits of a peace that has often been internationally sponsored, and undoubtedly hard fought for, so as to manage, an at times awkward, period of transition. From Colombia to Sierra Leone, Northern Ireland to South Africa, TJ has blossomed, being developed primarily in the 'Global North' but trialled, promoted, and enforced almost exclusively upon those living in the 'Global South'. Despite the existence of a vast array of critical TJ work, considering its (mis)application in the context of ongoing settler colonialism is one area that is conspicuous in its absence, albeit with a few notable exceptions (including breakthrough contributions from South African scholar Tshepo Madlingozi [2010] and more recent analyses offered by Park [2015, 2020]). It is also the case that there exists relatively little work analysing TJs role in enforcing the deeply flawed 'peace' agenda in Palestine, despite the region being subjected to unabated scholarly interest.

The convergence between TJ and peacebuilding has evolved to such an extent that the two have become almost synonymous, sharing much in terms of liberal, Eurocentric ideology, and enjoying the intellectual benefits that accompany becoming mainstreamed within the operational policies of the UN. When pressed into service in areas of ongoing settler colonial violence, such interventions, as I argue throughout this book, can have a deflating effect, particularly when they fail to properly platform the legitimate decolonial demands of an Indigenous community battling against attempts at their permanent erasure, as is the case of the Palestinians confronting violent Zionist settler colonialism. The scholarly contributions on the problematic role of international peacebuilding in the context of Palestine, in particular work that has examined the liberal foundations of the peacebuilding project, are vast and critical when it comes to highlighting the international community's catastrophic intervention and inaction in equal measure (see, for example: Haddad, 2018; Roy, 1995; Taghdisi-Rad, 2014; Turner, 2012; Turner & Kühn, 2015). In arguing that TJ interventions are cut from the same cloth, by extension the logic follows that, should they be uncritically promoted in the context of Palestine, they too have the potential to reinforce a deeply unjust status quo, whilst simultaneously side-lining meaningful conversations that must take place around decolonisation. It can further be argued that, if internationally sponsored and externally led, such interventions (should they remain silent on the need for an end to and reversal of ongoing Zionist settler colonialism) serve only to prioritise stability through conflict containment.

Transitional Justice and Peacebuilding

Often attributed to the pioneering work of Ruti Teitel (2000), TJ has evolved to such an extent that it has become a recognised methodology by the United Nations who have come to view it as an important sub-branch of its peacebuilding strategy. Teitel (2003: 69) considers TJ to amount to 'the conception of justice associated with periods of political change, characterised by legal responses to confront the wrongdoings of repressive predecessor regimes'. Its origins can be traced back to the end of the Second World War and the subsequent International Military Tribunals established at both Nuremberg and Tokyo, with the focus initially being on retributive, criminal justice for those considered to be most responsible for committing war-time atrocities. The intellectual energy around the sub-discipline gathered pace following the overthrowing of military dictatorships in South and Latin America and the subsequent push for democratisation led by the United States in the mid- to late 1980s. During a period of increased global uncertainty following the end of the Cold War, Western superpowers (led by the United States) sharpened their focus on those societies who had broken free from the shackles of autocracy and subsequently embraced or 'transitioned towards' more 'liberal' (read acceptable) Western democratic norms (Kritz, 1995; Teitel, 2003). In the 1990s, scholarly interest around TJ was energised by the ground-breaking work of the SATC which had sought to deal with South Africa's troubled past by engaging in a painful and very public process of truth recovery pertaining to the horrors of crimes committed during the apartheid regime (a process not without its critics, as noted in the previous chapter). The result has been the burgeoning development of a TJ orthodoxy, one that has been rigorously promoted by the West and assayed, primarily in 'transitioning' states in the 'Global South'. Sharp (2013: 174) notes that 'While definitions of transitional justice vary and have evolved over time, most of them attempt to capture a legal, political, and moral dilemma about how to deal with historic human rights violations and political violence in societies undergoing some form of political transition'. In providing his own summation of the core components of TJ, Khoury (2021: 154) notes that it comprises a 'variety of mechanisms, such as truth commissions, criminal trials, and apologies, whose purpose is to enable political reconciliation among competing parties in order to create a peaceful present and future'. So too Cavanaugh (2002: 934) who refers to TJ as a set of 'interim legal arrangements' designed to help fragile societies to move away from overt violent conflict, to 'conflict management'. This legalistic, rights-based focus is further evident in Peled and Rouhana's (2004: 320) definition, with the authors considering the role of TJ as being to 'seek to affirm and restore the dignity of those whose human rights have been violated, hold perpetrators accountable, emphasizing the harm they have done to individual human beings'. In this sense, TJ is a 'future-oriented' process, providing the tools to assist victims and survivors of past human rights abuses break free from the trauma and injustices of the past so as to ensure that their lived reality in the present day is one that is based on their dignity as human beings.

Despite continuing to evolve and grow over time, there are, broadly speaking, a number of core TJ concepts. This non-exhaustive list includes the pursuit of criminal prosecutions against those deemed most responsible for sanctioning gross human rights violations (a traditional judicial-led response that focuses on retributive justice targeting top-level actors); the pursuit of truth recovery (often through use of some form of truth commission responsible for investigating and reporting on key periods of human rights abuse so as to ensure a public record of what happened, when, and conclude who was ultimately responsible); reparations programmes (broadly conceived), including a mix of state-sponsored initiatives to promote repair for victims and survivors of past human rights abuses. These reparations packages vary considerably and often involve a complex balance when managing the needs of victims and survivors, those who require 'justice' versus the overall needs of society to move on, and often comprise some (or all) of the following: material compensation for victims and survivors, public apologies from newly installed political representatives, or other grassroots driven acts of commemorative practice, often with the aim of raising civic consciousness amongst the emergent state. A further key component in the TJ arsenal is institutional reform so as to ensure that the crucial aim of non-repetition of past abuses is secured. Institutional reform can involve a variety of processes, including security sector transformation, and a fundamental reformation of state-institutions (unsurprising when one considers the fact that it is often the corrupt emanations of the state, such as the military, the police, and the judiciary who played a lead role in sustaining the past repression of citizens). Institutional reform aims to ensure accountability for the newly installed, transitional government, to automatically enhance credibility and add further weight to the claim of 'never again'. Within these core, foundational TJ principles, a number of equally important issues have been considered across various post-conflict contexts, including issues pertaining to gender justice, challenging sexual and gender-based violence, and ensuring equal gender access to redress for past abuses.

By focusing on the needs of victims and survivors through consideration of issues such as: reparations for harm suffered, truth recovery, institutional reform, and reintegration of former combatants, the rather lofty aim of TJ is therefore to ensure that fragile peace processes in 'transitioning' societies are successfully embedded and thus afforded greater chance of long-term success. With the evolving nature of modern warfare, with fewer outright and decisive state-sponsored military victories (Kaldor, 2013), some scholarly energy has shifted towards considering whether TJ engagement in the midst of ongoing hostilities may aid the generation of a peaceful conclusion between adversaries, thus helping to kick-start a much-needed process of transition out of conflict (see, for example, Engstrom, 2013; Hansen, 2019; Unger & Wierda, 2009). When we consider that 'attempts at rendering justice for serious crimes increasingly occur' as Hansen (2019: 949) has argued 'not only after war has ended, but while it is still ongoing', this turn to focus on the increasingly nebulous boundary between TJ and other forms of peacebuilding is perhaps unsurprising. This convergence is highlighted by McAuliffe (2017) who has drawn attention to the fact that TJ has come to be recognised as an important component of any peacebuilding strategy, citing several reports from the UNGA and the UNSC that have been explicit on TJ's potential to help shift the climate on the ground in areas blighted by ongoing conflict. The wafer-thin divisions between the two have been the subject of further scholarly critiques from Sriram (2007), Sharp (2013), and McAuliffe (2017). In 'Mapping the Nexus of Transitional Justice and Peacebuilding', Baker and Obradovic-Wochnik (2016: 288) highlight:

> The 'turns' through which peacebuilding studies have gone in the 2000s and 2010s as peacebuilding practices have themselves evolved share a concern with scale, asymmetry and power which is also visible in critical studies of 'top-down' transitional justice. Critiques of the 'liberal peace' as an ineffective, inappropriate or outright neo-imperialist form of Western power projection in the name of peacebuilding (Pugh 2005; Chandler 2006; Cooper 2007; Richmond 2009b; Jabri 2012) echo the reaction against 'top-down' transitional justice mechanisms that characterizes much critical literature on the ICTY, the ICTR and the International Criminal Court.

In citing the work of Chandler (2010: 32), McAuliffe (2017) argues that this merging between the two practices is perhaps understandable in that 'traditional TJ exemplifies an ineluctable trend towards a form of liberal governmentality in which democracy and market economics represent the most efficacious route to peace, to the exclusion of redistribution and equality', a common charge levied against other forms of peacebuilding intervention. This argument is important in the present context in that, 'the peace that the West often talks about', according to Oliver Richmond (2004: 139) 'can be defined as a status quo that favours western hegemony by exporting its own structures of governance, economics, and norms seen as the only surviving approach to maintaining peace and order'. With the advent of globalisation, Western conflict interventionists—'peace-builders'—have developed a rich set of peacebuilding tools that can be bluntly exported to areas experiencing ongoing conflict (Richmond, 2004: 132). A similar trend has been discerned by Jamar (2019: 54) when it comes to the burgeoning development of a TJ orthodoxy:

Professional elites of transitional justice disseminate and consolidate a contentious normative framework that neglects (and hence reproduces) unequal power dynamics. From such perspectives, the transitional justice normative crusade enables token democracies to be consolidated and epistemic violence to be inflicted.

These 'professional elites', to borrow from Jamar (2019), include the UN, international NGOs, aid organisations, donors, the academy, and a whole host of policymakers (Sriram, 2007: 583) the very same organisations who have played a leading role in promoting a bastardised 'peace' in Palestine that has marginalised Palestinian decolonial demands and helped to sharpen and embolden ongoing Zionist settler colonialism. McAuliffe (2017: 93) further points to the fact that TJ and peacebuilding interventions share many of the same fundamental flaws in that, 'both... attempt to impose unfamiliar individualist rights-based solutions, securitized to the extent that they merely attempt to contain conflict, and conservative to the extent that these approaches preclude transforming conflicts by critically examining their basis'. None more so is that evident than in the case of Palestine. When we consider that, in the context of Palestine, the peacebuilding juggernaut (as elaborated on below), with its focus on economic (in)stability and flawed state building through internationally sponsored donor intervention, has failed to realise any meaningful decolonial 'justice' for Palestine, it ought to be with a hefty degree of scepticism that we choose to embrace a language and practice of TJ that shares many (if not all) of the same ideological underpinnings. The goal of any critical scholar focused on TJ should be to challenge the rationale of those organisations taking a lead role more carefully. Taken together, several important questions emerge: in an area where there has been no transition out of conflict, where settler colonial violence remains as sharp as ever against an Indigenous population, despite various attempts at internationally endorsed peacebuilding, what role is TJ assuming given it is intimately linked to a peacebuilding framework? In addition, if they are entertained, for whom and in whose interests are these TJ interventions best served?

Enforcing a Colonial 'Peace' on Palestine

Speaking on stage in Germany at an event entitled 'Hijacking Memory: The Holocaust and the New Right' leading Palestinian intellectual Tareq

Baconi presented the decades-long struggle of the Palestinian people against Zionist settler colonialism and the myriad 'justice' issues that every Palestinian holds as truth, the resolution of which remains central in the pursuit of any future decolonial peace:

> In 1948, the Zionist movement declared the creation of the State of Israel, and constituted itself as a regime of apartheid, committed to maintaining Jewish domination in Palestine. Since then, Israel has expanded its persistent colonization of Palestinian land and relentless dispossession of the Palestinian people, a dual process of land consolidation and demographic engineering. Today, Israel is an apartheid state with full sovereign control over all of Palestine, from the Jordan River to the Mediterranean Sea, persecuting the Palestinian people at home and in their exile. Every Palestinian carries these simple truths in their heart and bears witness to them on a daily basis.

Whilst the most formative phase in the modern period of colonial violence meted out against the Palestinian population can be traced back to the creation of the Israeli State in 1948, a process facilitated by willing partners that comprised the newly established United Nations (UN), when it comes to spotlighting the deeply problematic role played by the international community, one must reaffirm the impact of the disastrous Balfour declaration of 1917. Drafted by then British foreign secretary Arthur Balfour, the declaration stated publicly, for the first time, the British government's view that they considered it to be important, necessary, and ultimately 'just', that a 'national home for the Jewish people' be established in historic Palestine, adding a sense of international credibility (Perugini & Gordon, 2015) to the suggestion and providing the public support needed to ensure that Zionism's settler colonial aspirations could be realised, despite the obvious negative impact on the Indigenous Palestinian population. The division of historic Palestine following the end of the British Mandate and the subsequent intervention by the newly formed UN (by way of UNGA Res. 181) resulted in an uneven partition of the land, from the Jordan River to the Mediterranean Sea, with two-thirds assigned to the fledgling Israeli state, giving rise to the mass displacement of the Indigenous Palestinian population and birthing the world's longest running refugee crisis. Jerusalem was to receive special protected status as 'corpus separatum', effectively becoming an international city administered by the UN for an initial period of 10 years. Thus, from the outset, international intervention and attempts at resolving 'conflict'—one that had effectively been licenced by the international community—directly caused one of the most pressing 'justice' issues, one that remains unresolved to this day. Whilst partition of historic Palestine was resisted vehemently by the Indigenous Palestinian population, with support from neighbouring Arab allies and Palestinian resistance in exile, decisive Israeli victories (helped in no small part from military and logistical support provided by international partners, in particular the United States) resulted in the entrenchment and expansion of the Israeli state over large swathes of historic Palestine, including the West Bank of the River Jordan, the Gaza Strip, and East Jerusalem, the population of which remain subject to the ongoing scourge of violent Zionist settler colonial expansion through a combination of belligerent Israeli military occupation (in its various forms) and the imposition of an apartheid reality. From 1948 to 1967, with significant fiscal and military aid from abroad, Jewish migration to historic Palestine was greatly increased, allowing the fledgling Israeli state to consolidate its grip over the land, its resources, and the Indigenous Palestinian population. In combatting decades of Israeli state building (read colonisation), including the full annexation of the West Bank and Gaza Strip, the Golan Heights (Syria), and the Sheba'a Farms (Lebanon), Tartir (2015) notes that the 'Palestinians accumulated multiple cycles of contention and engaged in contentious collective actions to give birth to the Palestinian revolution (Al-Thawra Al-Filstiniya)'. Simultaneously, international diplomatic energy was focused on finding a 'solution', owing in no small part to the relative success of various Palestinian campaigns of civil disobedience and active armed resistance.

'For Palestinians waiting for justice' as Browne and Bradley (2021) have noted, the passing of 'time can be measured in subsequent peace processes – Wye River, Camp David, Oslo, Hebron, Taba, Beirut'. Of the various attempts, it is the signing of the Interim Agreement on the West Bank and Gaza Strip (also commonly referred to as the Oslo II Accord) that has been most impactful. Whilst heralded as a major breakthrough in terms of 'peacebuilding' by the international community (and by many on the ground), others have pointed to the fact that the Accords are yet further evidence of colonial intervention, imbued with bureaucratic restrictions and replete with limitations placed upon Palestinians in pursuit of self-determination (Dabed, 2021). Further partition and fragmentation of an already fractured geography remained the order of the day, with the land designated as 'Palestinian' sub-divided into Areas A,

B, and C, each with varying degrees of limited autonomy, and based on perceived Israeli security concerns. A generous description of the 1993 Oslo Accords would be to argue that their role was to act as a set of guiding principles which would eventually lead to eventual Palestinian statehood. In the short term, a hiatus in conflict-related violence gave the impression that their intervention had been relatively successful. However, in reality, as a mode of peacebuilding, Oslo provided 'another layer of counterinsurgency strategies designed to create an acquiescent Palestinian population' (Turner & Kühn, 2015: 154) further revealing that for all intents and purposes, it was conflict management, not resolutions based on justice, that would be the overriding strategy.

From the Accords was born the Palestinian National Authority (PA) the body designate to represent the voice of the Palestinian people, sidelining the Palestinian Liberation Organisation (PLO), and within it, those who opposed the Oslo 'Peace Process', turning former freedom fighters into 'docile colonial administrators' (Dabed, 2021). Whereas the PLO had been relatively successful in homogenising Palestinian resistance by uniting the diaspora—from those living in refugee camps in exile to those living under occupation in historic Palestine—the PA 'gutted the PLO politically' (Fatafta & Tartir, 2020). During the period of post-Oslo optimism, foreign aid flooded the West Bank and Gaza Strip, all in an effort to cement (no pun intended) perceived political gains and based on a belief that, a strong economic response with a focus on neoliberal growth and opportunities for jobs and perceived prosperity, would be enough to package and sell the limited decolonial reality that was on offer. 'The PA's place as the de facto Palestinian representative in relations with Israel and in the so-called peace process' (Fatafta & Tartir, 2020) was subsequently secured through vast injections of foreign aid and attendant international pressure. This form of liberal peacebuilding practice 'is based on the belief that it establishes the political, organisational and economic foundations for addressing, if not the roots of conflict, then at least the externalities' (Haddad, 2018: 25). The focus on issues such as security, law, and the markets was at the expense of addressing any number of justice issues that had the potential to be politically destabilising, with these awkward conversations kicked down the road, to be addressed at some (as yet undetermined) mythical period of time in the future. By outsourcing the economic growth and development of the future State of Palestine to the international donor community, those who were choosing to pick up the tab despite Israel's alleged responsibility as an occupying power, including the European Union (EU) and other international donors helped (and continue to) absolve the Israeli state of any responsibilities therein, whilst simultaneously delineating the boundaries of what a future resolution on the ground may ultimately look like. 'Western peacebuilding interventions' as Turner and Kühn (2015: 140) have argued, 'helped to create a political economy that stabilises from the inside - and so have played a key role in the creation and preservation of a violent colonial peace'. In addition, according to Taghdisi-Rad (2014: 22) under the Paris Protocol on Economic Relations, signed alongside the Oslo Accords, the proposed semi-autonomous Palestinian economy was completely tied and therefore dependent upon Israeli policies, rules, and regulations, further highlighting that Palestinian economic independence was deemed secondary to Israeli economic needs. This internationally sponsored neoliberal 'development' practice has entered a new phase with the rigorous promotion of 'resilience' programmes (Keelan & Browne, 2020; Richter-Devroe, 2011; Ryan, 2015) designed to ensure on-the-ground gains in the absence of a meaningful and successful post-conflict transition. Packaging international aid and financial assistance as development serves the dual purpose of (a) coercing Palestinian compliance (by placing conditions upon those who benefit from this form of support), whilst simultaneously (b) sowing the seeds of fragmentation between those who choose to engage with the only offer on the table—peace-lite—versus those who prefer to disassociate and continue the struggle, by rejecting the various, deeply unjust compromises that are demanded.

During the Oslo deliberations, a number of high-profile issues were negotiated 'off the table' considered too contentious to be resolved at the time, including the final borders of any future Palestinian (and Israeli) state, the status of Jerusalem, and perhaps most pressingly, the right of return for Palestinian refugees hoping to settle in historic Palestine. Thus, from the outset, the most significant attempt at making 'peace' failed to countenance that the injustice meted out against the Indigenous Palestinian population was rooted in a legacy of experiencing Zionist settler colonial displacement, one that benefits from the support of a complicit international community, and which ultimately defines the parameters for resolution. Whilst the refugee issue has been central to the manner by which the question of Palestine has been considered by the international community since 1948, the response of the international community has been to view refugees and their displacement as being that of a humanitarian crisis (Imseis, 2020). This is crucial as it yet further reveals the manner in which international law has operated against the decolonial aspirations of the Palestinians (as discussed in greater detail in Chapter 4). By choosing to unburden themselves of the responsibility for resolving the refugee issue through the application of established principles of international law, organs such as the UN have 'conflict managed' the complexities that arise from the forcible transfer of an Indigenous people, treating it as a humanitarian, rather than a legal issue, further marginalising their own role in helping to sponsor ongoing Israeli settler colonialism. Concurrently, in choosing to blindly finance the illusion of a Palestinian state with all the traditionally associated neoliberal trappings, the international community have 'embedded Palestinian vulnerability under the duplicity of Western governments and donors who remain willing to blindly subsidise a vulnerable Palestinian economy rather than provide any real attempt to redress the occupation for fear of the political repercussions' (Keelan & Browne, 2020: 6).

In the post-Oslo era, the international community has become further embroiled in the world of Palestinian political affairs, choosing who it considers to be the 'acceptable' representatives of the Palestinian population living under occupation in the West Bank and Gaza Strip, and in so doing, ignoring a democratic process that returned a set of electoral results deemed problematic. The result has been the further fragmentation of an already dislocated polity and the emergence of an intra-factional conflict between the two largest parties, President Mahmoud Abbas's Fateh and the Islamist group, Hamas. A curious governing reality has thus emerged, one that endures in the present day, with the West Bank controlled by Fateh and the Gaza Strip, by Hamas. According to Fatafta and Tartir (2020), one of the primary reasons the PA remain in a position of relative power, despite the fact that it has almost no independent political decision-making capacity, is due to the fact that it remains totally dependent on the financial and political will of an international community who refuse to countenance its collapse for fear of the subsequent breakdown in the security coordination with the Israelis. Such criticism has led to accusations of the PA being little more than enforcers of the Israeli occupation, as noted by Dabed (2021) above, with Bahdi and Kassis (2016: 2) pointing out that this is 'the quintessential example of neo-colonialism at work'. Since Oslo, Palestinians continue to encounter the everyday violence of Zionist settler colonialism, including being subjected to varying degrees of actual and structural violence. The construction of a 'Separation Wall' in 2002 has had a catastrophic impact on the ground, with Palestinian towns and cities yet further fragmented and Palestinian arable land used for grazing and growing crops confiscated. The Wall has, in effect, allowed for a de facto annexation of the West Bank, tracking deep into areas of land supposedly reserved for any future Palestinian state. Those who live in the Gaza Strip have borne the brunt of the failings of Oslo, with catastrophic levels of violence meted out by the Israeli Army during four separate wars (2008, 2012, 2014 and 2021) accompanied by a siege warfare that, at the time of writing, is well into its 15th year. Across the West Bank and East Jerusalem, violent settler colonial expansion is further evident through the continued growth of illegal Israeli settlements, with the attendant confiscation and destruction of Palestinian land, and the forcible displacement of the Palestinian population in both urban and rural settings. The building of a 'settler only' infrastructure and subsequent increase in Israeli manned checkpoints designed to monitor and stifle Palestinian movement fits well within the widely understood definition and logic of settler colonialism. Therefore, in every aspect of life, control of the Indigenous Palestinian population remains with the coloniser, physically managed through a deeply embedded colonial architecture, accompanied by attempts to crackdown on expressions of dissent and outward acts of both violent and nonviolent resistance. In addition, the 'gradual erosion of the PA's legitimacy' amongst the Palestinian population, as Tartir (2015: 469) notes, has fostered an 'authoritarian trend in the PA's character and in the operations of its security forces'. The potential collapse of the PA's hegemonic position amongst the Palestinian population in general, and the capacity for societal breakdown, will perhaps cause most disquiet amongst those who have blindly sponsored the 'peace process' up until this point. Despite international protestations to the contrary, and the constant towing of the diplomatic party line, the only 'peace' that has ever been on offer in and for Palestine is one that maintains the deep asymmetry that characterises the relationship between oppressor and oppressed. Every iteration of the 'peacebuilding' process has been premised on Palestinian concession rather than a focus on reversing the ceaseless scourge of violent Zionist settler colonial expansion and attempts at Palestinian erasure. If there is a role for the international community to play (which in and of itself is debatable when we consider its track record to date), it must be to quash these asymmetries and to engage in a proper re-evaluation of its relationship in providing an inoculative veneer of credibility for a state that is hell bent on completing its settler colonialist aspirations. Thus, if we accept that there has been a seamless confluence between TJ and peacebuilding practice, this must be the logical starting point for any critical scholar who wishes to make a serious case for engaging in TJ work in and for Palestine.

Conclusion

As a 'deeply contested concept' (Khoury, 2021: 153), the capacity for TJ 'to devise real alternatives to the failed peace process' will live or die on whether it chooses to address the issue of decolonisation in historic Palestine or if it falls back on its liberal peacebuilding preference for 'conflict management', engaging in cursory consideration of a select number of tokenistic issues related to the past whilst failing to consider the foundational and enduring violence of Zionist settler colonialism. 'Beyond the resonances of 'transition' in an individual context' as Baker and Obradovic-Wochnik (2016: 287) argue 'discourses of transition in any setting imply assumptions about 'what the transition is "from" and "to"' which often go unvoiced but need to be critically examined (Bell and O'Rourke, 2007: 35)'. In the context of Palestine, where there has been constant international intervention, which in turn has allowed for the embedding and expansion of Zionist settler colonialism—where the 'transitions' have been imposed through a process of Western-sponsored peacebuilding practices and where the transitions have been from various colonial powers at the expense of Palestinian freedom and autonomy—the blunt imposition of TJ, as an ideological extension of this peacebuilding model, replete with its liberal tendencies, only serves to embed and engrain injustice. Any TJ in and for Palestine, therefore, must be 'incorporated into a larger political project that seeks to establish equality and justice for all Palestinians' (Khoury, 2021: 153). The lack of a meaningful 'political transition' and the confusion over what this 'political project' amounts to means that Palestine therefore 'represents a unique transitional site' (Bahdi & Kassis, 2020: 199).

Reflecting on his work in Uganda, Branch (2014: 612/613) argues that TJ 'can be counter-revolutionary when it silences demands for justice that transgress the liberal framework (Meister, 2011)… [and] conservative when it reinforces structures of domination and inequality in the name of reconciliation and forgiveness'. Thus, when it comes to the case of Palestine, it is important that TJ avoids becoming 'A way of managing natives, not of organizing or enabling native agency' (Roberts, 2020). If it is genuine in its desire to assist in spotlighting a 'justice'-oriented decolonial future in historic Palestine, TJ interventions can never be driven by those who enjoy positions of privilege within the settler colonial apparatus, nor those who have sponsored the failed peacebuilding project thus far. If they are, they will always suffer a legitimacy crisis. This in turn necessitates the raising of serious questions around the way in which TJ interventions in Palestine are actively promoted and championed by international actors, including the UN. The growth of an emerging scholarship that has begun to assess whether or not TJ practices can be a useful framework when seeking to address 'injustice perpetrated against indigenous peoples under regimes of settler colonialism that are also established liberal democracies' (Park, 2020: 260) opens up possibilities for theorists and practitioners interested in challenging the rationale for TJ that takes place in sites of ongoing settler colonial violence. However, as will be shown in the following chapters, in many instances, the praxis, language, and application of TJ in Palestine have been subjected to forms of colonial management that mirrors other peacebuilding practices that have been weaponised over the course of decades of flawed international engagement. In this sense, the 'liberal' teleology (Park, 2020) of TJ serves to marginalise and stigmatise legitimate anti-colonial resistance by redirecting energy towards standalone, detached 'justice' issues that are considered in isolation from a broader decolonial requirement. It therefore remains to be seen if a radical turn in the maturation of the sub-discipline is possible, or (as I suspect), TJ that takes places in areas of ongoing settler colonial 'conflict, becomes a useful form of subterfuge, providing the ruse of 'justice' for a few and kicking the decolonial can further down the road.

References

Bahdi, R., & Kassis, M. (2016). Decolonisation, dignity and development aid: A judicial education experience in Palestine. *Third World Quarterly, 37*(11), 2010–2027.

Bahdi, R., & Kassis, M. (2020). Institutional trustworthiness, transformative judicial education and transitional justice: A Palestinian experience. In *Transitional justice in comparative perspective* (pp. 185–215). Palgrave Macmillan.

Baker, C., & Obradovic-Wochnik, J. (2016). Mapping the nexus of transitional justice and peacebuilding. *Journal of Intervention and Statebuilding, 10*(3), 281–301.

Bell, C., & O'Rourke, C. (2007). Does feminism need a theory of transitional justice? An introductory essay. *The International Journal of Transitional Justice, 1*(1), 23–44.

Branch, A. (2014). The violence of peace: Ethnojustice in Northern Uganda. *Development and Change, 45*(3), 608–630. https://doi.org/10.1111/dech.12094

Browne, B. C., & Bradley, E. (2021). Promoting Northern Ireland's peacebuilding experience in Palestine–Israel: Normalising the status quo. *Third World Quarterly, 42*(7), 1625–1643.

Cavanaugh, K. A. (2002). Selective justice: The case of Israel and the occupied territories. *Fordham International Law Journal, 26*, 934.

Chandler, D. (2010). The 'liberal peace' critique of international intervention. In *International statebuilding* (pp. 32–52). Routledge.

Dabed, E. (2021). The Oslo agreements and the Palestinian authority: Or how to convert freedom fighters into docile colonial administrators. *Confluences Mediterranee, 117*(2), 161–175.

Engstrom, P. (2013). Transitional justice and ongoing conflict. In *Transitional justice and peacebuilding on the ground: Victims and ex-combatants* (pp. 41–61). Routledge.

Fatafta, M., & Tartir, A. (2020). Why Palestinians need to reclaim the PLO. *Foreign Policy.* https://foreignpolicy.com/2020/08/20/palestinians-reclaimplo-palestinian-authority-democracy/

Haddad, T. (2018). *Palestine Ltd.: Neoliberalism and nationalism in the occupied territory.* Bloomsbury.

Hansen, T. O. (2019). Opportunities and challenges seeking accountability for war crimes in Palestine under the International Criminal Court's complementarity regime. *Notre Dame Journal of International & Comparative Law, 9*, 1.

Imseis, A. (2020). Negotiating the illegal: On the United Nations and the illegal occupation of Palestine, 1967–2020. *European Journal of International Law, 31*(3), 1055–1085.

Jamar, A. (2019). The crusade of transitional justice tracing the journeys of hegemonic claims. In *Violence and democracy* (pp. 53–59). The British Academy.

Kaldor, M. (2013). In defence of new wars. *Stability: International Journal of Security and Development, 2*(1). https://doi.org/10.5334/sta.at

Keelan, E. P., & Browne, B. C. (2020). Problematising resilience: Development practice and the case of Palestine. *Development in Practice, 30*(4), 459–471.

Khoury, N. (2021). Transitional justice in Palestine/Israel: Whose justice? Which transition? In L. Farsakh (Ed.), *Rethinking statehood in Palestine.* University of California Press. https://doi.org/10.1525/luminos.113.g

Kritz, N. J. (Ed.). (1995). *Transitional justice: How emerging democracies reckon with former regimes* (Vol. 3). US Institute of Peace Press.

Madlingozi, T. (2010). On transitional justice entrepreneurs and the production of victims. *Journal of Human Rights Practice, 2*(2), 208–228.

McAuliffe, P. (2017). The marginality of transitional justice within liberal peacebuilding: Causes and consequences. *Journal of Human Rights Practice, 9*(1), 91–103.

Park, A. S. J. (2015). Settler colonialism and the politics of grief: Theorising a decolonising transitional justice for Indian residential schools. *Human Rights Review, 16*(3), 273–293.

Park, A. S. J. (2020). Settler colonialism, decolonization and radicalizing transitional justice. *International Journal of Transitional Justice, 14*(2), 260–279.

Peled, Y., & Rouhana, N. N. (2004). Transitional justice and the right of return of the Palestinian refugees. *Theoretical Inquiries in Law, 5*(2), 317–332.

Perugini, N., & Gordon, N. (2015). *The human right to dominate*. Oxford University Press.

Richmond, O. P. (2004). The globalization of responses to conflict and the peacebuilding consensus. *Cooperation and Conflict, 39*(2), 129–150.

Richter-Devroe, S. (2011). Palestinian women's everyday resistance: Between normality and normalisation. *Journal of International Women's Studies, 12*(2), 32–46.

Roberts, R. S. (2020). How 'transitional justice' colonized South Africa's TRC. *Modern Languages Open*. https://doi.org/10.3828/mlo.v0i0.318

Roy, S. M. (1995). *The Gaza Strip: The political economy of de-development*. Institute for Palestine Studies.

Ryan, C. (2015). Everyday resilience as resistance: Palestinian women practicing sumud. *International Political Sociology, 9*(4), 299–315.

Sharp, D. N. (2013). Interrogating the peripheries: The preoccupations of fourth generation transitional justice. *Harvard Human Rights Journal, 26*, 149.

Sriram, C. L. (2007). Justice as peace? Liberal peacebuilding and strategies of transitional justice. *Global Society, 21*(4), 579–591.

Taghdisi-Rad, S. (2014). The economic strategies of occupation: Confining development and buying-off peace. In *Decolonizing Palestinian political economy* (pp. 13–31). Palgrave Macmillan.

Tartir, A. (2015). Contentious economics in occupied Palestine. In *Contentious politics in the Middle East* (pp. 469–499). Palgrave Macmillan.

Teitel, R. G. (2000). *Transitional justice*. Oxford University Press on Demand.

Teitel, R. G. (2003). Transitional justice genealogy. *Harvard Human Rights Journal, 16*, 69.

Turner, M. (2012). Completing the circle: Peacebuilding as colonial practice in the occupied Palestinian territory. *International Peacekeeping, 19*(4), 492–507.

Turner, M., & Kühn, F. P. (2015). Securing and stabilising: Peacebuilding as counterinsurgency in the occupied Palestinian territory. In M. Turner & F. P. Kühn (2016), *The politics of international intervention*. Routledge.

Unger, T., & Wierda, M. (2009). Pursuing justice in ongoing conflict: A discussion of current practice. In *Building a future on peace and justice* (pp. 263–302). Springer.

CHAPTER 3

Truth, Acknowledgement, and Combatting 'Memoricide'

Abstract Truth recovery that takes place against the backdrop of settler colonialism ought to be focused on combating violent state-sponsored attempts at erasure by ensuring that Indigenous loss and trauma at the hands of the settler is common knowledge. The way that the truth is curated must involve supporting activities that reinforce native identity, history, and presence on the land. However, and taking this one step further, as this chapter argues by reference to existing grassroots attempts at truth recovery in Palestine, it is simply not enough to platform the revelation of uncomfortable truths or to provide opportunities for settler violence of the past to be 'confessed' in public if it is disassociated from challenging the present-day structures of ongoing oppression.

Keywords Truth recovery · Erasure · Zochrot · Revelation

> Until lions have their own historians, tales of the hunt shall always glorify the hunter.
>
> Chinua Achebe

Introduction

The role of the Israeli state in attempting to bury unwanted 'truths' about its past, including primarily the foundational violence that accompanied its declaration of independence in 1948 at the expense of the forced displacement of some 750,000 Indigenous Palestinians, has fostered the emergence of a grassroots TJ movement across the region whose focus has been on combating 'memoricide'. Defined as the concerted effort to eradicate Palestine from history through an insidious process of state-sponsored, Zionist settler colonial erasure of Palestinian identity, history, heritage, and culture (Lentin, 2013; Masalha, 2012), the aim of 'memoricide' is to expunge the 'history of one people in order to write that of another people's over it' (Pappé, 2007: 231). Such a process makes sense when we recall that settler colonialism's 'logic of elimination' (Wolfe, 2006) requires the indigenous population to disappear (Veracini, 2013) both literally and figuratively. Beyond outright attempts at elimination of the native, processes of erasure often occur primarily through Indigenous assimilation or by the promotion of widespread, state-sponsored amnesia (Park, 2015). The role of truth-based TJ in such settler colonial contexts ought to be focused on combating these violent state-sponsored attempts at erasure by ensuring that Indigenous loss and trauma at the hands of the settler is common knowledge, not merely buried in the annals of the past. According to Park (2015, 2020) and Nagy (2022), this form of truth recovery practice should also involve supporting activities that reinforce native identity, history, and presence on the land. However, and taking this one step further, it is simply not enough to allow for the revelation of uncomfortable truths or to provide opportunities for the settler violence of the past to be 'confessed' in public if it is somehow disassociated from challenging the present-day structures of ongoing oppression that allow for the maintenance of an unjust status quo. 'Genuine remembrance' as we are reminded by Asmal et al. (1997: 13) 'must renounce the hangman in order to celebrate the innocents hanged'.

Popularised through the pioneering, albeit fundamentally flawed (as outlined earlier) work of the South African TRC, engagement in processes of 'truth recovery' following a period of conflict has come to be seen as a key aim of fledgling states when attempting to strengthen societal cohesion and disassociate present-day governance from the violence of their predecessor(s). Arguments abound pertaining to the purported cathartic role of truth revelation in alleviating victim/survivor trauma, including the extent to which full disclosure about past human rights abuses can ultimately provide the much sought-after line in the sand needed for any society to fully move on. 'Common wisdom' as Priscilla Hayner (2002: 30) has suggested 'holds that the future depends on the past: one must confront the legacy of past horrors or there will be no foundation on which to build a new society'. However, when the 'new' society in question requires the complete erasure of an existing, Indigenous one, fulsome revelation of past horrors is often politically destabilising and thus less than ideal. In the absence of a period of transition, and in the context of ongoing settler colonial erasure in historic Palestine, centring the 'truth' around the foundational violence that undergirds and maintains the Zionist state-building project assumes great significance and is linked, one could argue, to the very concept of Palestinian survival. Since the formation of the State, successive Israeli governments have invested great time, energy, and resources into marginalising the narrative of Palestinian dispossession and exile, all in an effort to, for the most part, delegitimise claims associated with the right of return. This has been done through, *inter alia*, a combination of: (a) ignoring it completely, (b) providing counter-narratives that centre on Palestinian flight rather than forced exile, and by (c) criminalising those involved in commemorating and recounting narratives of the Nakba to a wider public audience (Lentin, 2013; Masalha, 2012; Pappé, 2007). Bracka (2017) draws particular attention to the role played by the Israeli legal system in seeking to delegitimise and/or criminalise revelations of the truth behind the Nakba, noting how 'Israeli laws and legal institutions reproduce denial of the Palestinians past, refraining from addressing the rights of Palestinian refugees, particularly the right of return, and thus reifying the silencing of this issue in the public space' (2017: 358). Israeli judicial suppression of the Nakba has also extended into the realm of passing legal judgements on cultural production, most notably in relation to films that have engaged with promoting interpretations of events that transpired in 1948. 'To embark on a truth recovery process', as Marie Breen-Smyth (2007: 39) has noted, 'is profoundly politically challenging'. It is against the urgent backdrop of continued attempts at Palestinian erasure that a grassroots NGO community engaged in bottom-up truth recovery praxis has emerged.

In considering what role truth recovery mechanisms *ought* to play in combatting Zionist settler colonialisms attempts at Indigenous erasure, the views of Park (2015) and her analysis of Judith Butler's (2006) thesis on grievable life act as particularly useful anchoring points. In the context of settler colonial violence, Park (2015: 274) maintains, TJ 'must engage a "politics of grief", which is addressed to both dimensions of decolonisation'. Reflecting on historic settler colonial violence and truth recovery in reference to the Indian Residential School system in Canada, the aim of TJ ought to be on ensuring that 'Indigenous life' is rendered grievable, which, she argues, strikes 'at the heart of the settler colonial logic of elimination'. Alongside this need to safeguard Indigenous life, TJ in such settler colonial contexts must ensure that 'the politics of grief resists a purely emotional or affective understanding of grief that lends itself to settlers simply "feeling bad" for colonial violence. Rather, grief must be understood as a political resource that calls for an agenda of decolonising structural justice' (Park, 2015: 274).

The violence of Zionist settler colonialism subjects the Palestinian population to a range of policies and practices that seek to render Indigenous life irrelevant, invisible, and ultimately 'ungrievable' (Butler, 2006). 'Ungrievability', as Park (2015) summarises, is premised on the derealisation of some lives as not quite life, not quite human, rendered 'destructible', 'lose-able' or subject to forfeiture, 'precisely because they are framed as being already lost or forfeited' (Butler, 2009: 31, as cited in Park, 2015: 279).

> In a state of settler colonialism, Indigenous life is not recognised as life but as something to be ridden from settler space. From the perspective of settler colonialism, for instance, an Indigenous language irretrievably lost does not qualify as loss because it was already marked for elimination... The tenacity of Indigenous life (by which I mean the survival, renewal, and vibrancy, against all odds, of Indigenous peoples, their cultures and traditions through resistance and struggle, which Veracini (2011: 8) posits as the basis of a postcolonial society), is met with a perpetual project of negation, which reminds us of the structural rather than once-and-for-all character of invasion. (Park, 2015: 279–280)

By linking together, the logic of settler colonialism and Butler's theory of ungrievable life, Park (2015) proposes that the role of truth recovery that takes place in such contexts ought to be to ensure that Indigenous life is elevated to the status of being worthy of grief which in turn can help in beginning a process of meaningful decolonisation and repairing the harm. Therefore, in considering the aims of TJ practices associated with truth recovery in the context of Palestine, there is a need to challenge this logic of elimination and in so doing, individuals and groups engaged in truth recovery processes—those who primarily emanate from the grassroots NGO sector across the region—must focus on action that stems the revisionist tide. In other words, all acts of truth recovery must be in service to combatting attempted processes of 'memoricide' (Masalha, 2012) and must seek ways of ensuring that Palestinian life is equally viewed as grievable. Delegitimising the narrative underpinning the historical existence of an Indigenous Palestinian population is one of the 'softer' (but no less nefarious) means of attempted erasure used by the settler state when seeking to retain its hegemonic stranglehold over Palestinian life. Narratives of the past are manipulated, controlled, and distorted so as to discredit them, evidence of a Palestinian presence on the land pre-1948 is physically destroyed (or built over), public acts of commemoration of the Palestinian Nakba are prohibited, Palestinian centres of art, culture, and heritage that point to Indigeneity are targeted, and a process of de-Arabisation (and by extension enacting processes of Judaization) takes place in traditionally Palestinian spaces (most notably in the Old City of Jerusalem). Alongside these attempts at erasure is the promotion of Israeli citizenship and the forced assimilation of the Indigenous Palestinian population into the Israeli state (through citizenship requirements and the implementation of legislation linked to oaths of allegiance).

Counter memoricide practices broadly mirroring examples of truth recovery TJ in other contexts have emerged, from a grassroots level, across historic Palestine, initiated by a combination of Palestinian and Israeli/Palestinian activist-led NGOs. Thus, ensuring that despite attempts to erase it from modern memory, the Palestinian Nakba remains omnipresent in the settler (Israeli) society. Through a combination of public facing events, online databases, digitisation of destroyed villages, and the promotion of narratives that run counter to the dominant Israeli state-sponsored one, the attempted memoricide of the Indigenous Palestinian presence is challenged and the trauma and legacy of the Nakba is kept alive. This truth recovery TJ work conducted by such organisations ensures that Palestinian life and loss are rendered 'grievable' providing a strong rebuttal to settler colonial attempts at eradication. All of which helps to 'reconstitute Indigenous people's individual and collective, literal and figurative deaths as loss, and thus assert that Indigenous life/lives matter' (Park, 2015: 286). Revelations around the violence that accompanied the formation of the Israeli state in 1948 at the expense of the forced displacement of the indigenous Palestinian population have long been 'uncovered' by Palestinian and Israeli activists, academics (including historians, geographers, and archivists), and more recently a range of local NGOs. The unlocking of previously hidden military archives and the gathering together of witness testimonies from surviving Israeli soldiers who oversaw forced expulsions and massacres of the Palestinian population have, in some sense, helped to unmask the 'truth'. However, in so doing, what has also become clear is that such revelations of crimes committed in the past, including the wholesale destruction of Palestinian villages and the murder of the Indigenous Palestinians writ large, can be 'revealed' in such a way since, at present, there is little at stake when it comes to ensuring criminal accountability or shifting the everyday reality on the ground. As Seth Anziska (2022) has argued, there can now be 'confession without consequence' and the 'possibility of exoneration without accountability' all of which, he suggests, reveals much about the fundamental moral decay that lies at the heart of Israeli society.

If those involved in unpacking the 'truth' about the past fail to meaningfully agitate for practical conversations around decolonisation, then their work falls into the category of being liberally irrelevant. Truth recovery without the requisite focus on reparations, institutional reform, Palestinian return, and meaningful decolonisation serves only to salve the conscience of the offender rather than providing justice for the victim. The emergence of grassroots organisations—both Israeli and Palestinian—engaged in formal and ad hoc truth recovery processes, I argue, also reveals a certain tension when it comes to issues regarding narration, and the extent to which the revelation of historical truths can be adequately led by members of the settler community. Furthermore, the extent to which TJ practices linked to truth recovery are capable of generating meaningful and constructive conversations on how to halt, reverse, and repair the damage done in the present day remains subject to debate. Such questions have been raised previously by Broadhead (2020: 339) in her analysis of the Israeli NGO most visibly associated with truth recovery practice in historic Palestine, *Zochrot* (alongside several other Israeli organisations). She asks:

> What is the role of the occupier in acknowledging past and present injustice? What role is there for settlers to act as allies to those dispossessed by colonial actions? Is it appropriate for settlers to participate in the telling of colonial history, and is it possible to do this without becoming the central character in the narrative?

In spotlighting some of these tensions, the aim here is to stimulate a broader conversation around the role of truth recovery practices that take place in spaces of ongoing settler colonialism and to critique what role, if any, the settler community ought to play when narrating 'truth' surrounding loss and trauma of the colonised. In borrowing from Edward Said's (1984) 'Permission to narrate' thesis and from more recent critiques offered by those who have queried the rationale and appropriateness of Palestinian 'truths' being legitimised or amplified when curated through the words and work of the coloniser, I seek to demonstrate that revelation for revelation's sake can, in many ways, be counterproductive. The extent to which these processes amount to 'truth recovery' or 'truth management', I argue, depends greatly on whether their aim is to stimulate proper debate around what ought to amount to actual, material, and structural decolonisation in Palestine. Should these uncovering of uncomfortable truths fail to be matched with strategies around reversal, the praxis, no matter how noble an enterprise, will be exposed to the same critique as other forms of TJ interventions; that they are ultimately the extension of the peacebuilding model that fails to agitate for decolonial 'justice'. Recovery of the 'truth' when it takes place in ongoing spaces of settler colonial erasure must centre on reclamation, not only of distorted historical narratives or of past traumas, but also of a decolonial future that is both meaningful and implementable.

Foundational myths and challenged narratives lie at the heart of the so-called Arab Israeli 'conflict' (Khoury, 2016), with native claims to the land framed as 'contested' or 'disputed' and selective 'truths' ingrained in mainstream (including international) discourse. Competing claims over the existence of an indigenous population, dating back to biblical times, are routinely offered as reasons for the justification of policies and practices in the present. 'The Zionist narrative' pertaining to indigeneity and connection to the land, as Nadim Khoury (2016) argues, 'is premised on the religious and ethnic link between the ancient Israelites and the modern Israelis. This continuous link was disrupted when the Jewish people were sent into exile'. Amara and Hawari (2019) suggest that 'Whilst Zionist settler colonialism shares all the hallmarks of European invasion, attempted superiority, and domination it simultaneously advances a nativist claim that suggests that Zionist returnees are just that; returnees to Palestine based on biblical narratives'. The persistent and closely held 'truth' for many Zionists is that Palestine was an empty, barren space in 1882, with the native Palestinians who resided there largely invisible (Pappé, 2007). Such a view is, as Nadera Shalhoub-Kevorkian (2015: 5) suggests, a highly spurious slur and an effort to 'reinforce the claim that Palestinians were/are not a people'. It is the fervently maintained incompatibility of an historical and deeply engrained Palestinian indigenous presence with Zionism's settler colonial aspirations that has led to competing attempts at revealing and suppressing historical truths and the birth of a grassroots TJ movement focused on truth recovery.

For most Palestinians, as Tareq Baconi (2022) states, the incontrovertible 'truth' when it comes to Palestine centres on the fact that, as a 'settler colonial movement', Zionism is 'intent on, at best, our erasure, and at worst, elimination. It is a racist ideology rooted in the belief of Jewish supremacy in Palestine'. Therefore, the role of the settler state in this regard is to work intentionally towards burying awkward historical 'truths', doing so by ensuring that difficult, unpalatable, or contentious accounts of past historic settler colonial violence are either completely suppressed or received in public with limited outcry (within both the settler and international communities). Challenging this obfuscation of the 'truth' is thus a core aim of those who seek to avail of TJ in the context of Palestine. As has been established from the outset, any conversation around 'justice' in Palestine curated through the apparatus of truth recovery must ensure careful attention is paid to nomenclature. If they shirk the language of settler colonialism, TJ practitioners and scholars who engage in truth recovery demonstrate a liberal bias, one that seeks to maintain, rather than disrupt the status quo, providing a veneer of 'justice' for a few whilst allowing for settler colonial expansion to continue unchecked. Worse still, if they are silent on the possibility of decolonisation, truth recovery interventions are toothless, playing an insidious role in enabling and facilitating the erasure of a Palestinian identity, the goal of the Zionist settler colonial project. Moreover, should such truth recovery interventions in Palestine '… adopt a technocratic discourse that silences other voices and inherent political battles while diverting attention from contemporary use of violence and oppression towards political opponents' (Jamar, 2019: 59), they will ultimately be acting in service of the settler at the expense of the colonised.

Recovering the Nakba

Writing in *The Electronic Intifada*, Pappé (2018) notes that: 'A deconstruction of Israel's approved history is the best way to challenge a word laundrette that turns ethnic cleansing into self-defence, land robbery into redemption and apartheid practices into "security" concerns'. The presentation of historical 'truths' in the context of Zionist settler colonialism in Palestine involves the politics of denial. The position of the Israeli state since its formation has been to attempt to bury the past literally, physically, and metaphorically by, either: permanently shuttering access to military archives that would be home to sensitive documentation on the events that transpired, building over destroyed Palestinian villages in an effort to hide the evidence of Palestinian inhabitation, and/or criminalising grassroots groups involved in promoting the truth behind the Nakba, one that runs counter to the narrative of the state. The end of the British Mandate in Palestine and the subsequent declaration of independence and formation of the Israeli State on 15th May 1948 is an event that is celebrated by the vast majority of Israeli's and one that is simultaneously commemorated by almost all Palestinians. The 'truth' surrounding the details pertaining to Zionist settler colonial violence, including fulsome revelations regarding the level and nature of violence that was meted out, remains subject to competing scholastic views. Leading Palestinian intellectuals have long since established how events that transpired in 1948 were part of a systemic and coordinated attempt to eradicate an Arab presence in historical Palestine (Khalidi, 2005; Masalha, 2012), yet Zionist counter-rhetoric presents the issue of Palestinian displacement at the time as being the result of several factors, including Pan-Arab aggression and a lack of confidence in their own leadership. If the Palestinian population left their homes and villages, or so the narrative goes, it was a voluntary decision based on a belief that they would be temporarily absent. In keeping with this Zionist line of argument, Karsh (2010: 3) reiterates the claim, suggesting that it was Palestinian flight, not expulsion, that created the birth of the Palestinian refugee problem, further suggesting that, '…Palestinians evacuated their country… not out of cowardice, but because they had lost all confidence in the existing system of defence… they had perceived its weakness, and realized the disequilibrium between their resources and organisation, and those of the Jews'. The Zionist position pertaining to Palestinian flight, one that has been mainstreamed as the 'truth' by successive Israeli governments, is an important foundation principle when seeking to mitigate and limit the criticism levied against the Israeli state in the present day. Moreover, as Josh Ruebner (2022), writing for the *Middle East Institute*, has noted: 'Nakba denial simultaneously serves as a mechanism to bolster Israel's denial of Palestinian refugee rights, to whitewash Israel's dispossession of Palestinians, to obfuscate Israel's eliminationist origins, and to encloak Israel's establishment in an ahistorical, virtuous narrative'. Burying the truth further serves the settler colonial aspirations of Zionism in that it helps to ensure that the thorny issue of the right of return for Palestinian refugees is avoided altogether.

In an effort to counter this state-sponsored version of the 'truth', in the mid- to late 1980s, a group of Israeli scholars published a series of 'monographs challenging the Israeli/Zionist narrative of the 1948 war that led to the dispossession and expulsion of three-quarters of a million Palestinians and the destruction of more than five hundred villages and localities in what had been Mandate Palestine' (Pappé, 2020: 22). Acknowledging that the work that underpinned and informed these 'new histories' had long been advanced by Palestinian scholars, Pappé (2020: 22) argues that what was different was the fact that the claims made were:

> Substantiated by declassified archival material. The research made possible by such material, which constitutes the main contribution of the New Historians' historiographical effort, categorically refuted a foundational Israeli propaganda claim that during what Israel calls its "War of Independence," the Palestinians left their homes voluntarily to make way for the invading Arab armies coming to their rescue, thus becoming refugees by their own hands.

Referring specifically to the erasure of the Nakba in the Israeli archives, Anziska (2019: 67) notes that '…in an Orwellian act of self-censorship that began in the early 2000s, the Defence Ministry's secretive security department, Malmab, spearheaded efforts to reclassify documents and methodically remove files from various archives across Israel to hide evidence of Israeli responsibility for the Nakba'. Such acts of truth management make perfect sense in spaces of ongoing colonial violence in that it allows for the smooth continuation of the present-day process of settler colonial erasure in Palestine, undeterred by any duty to address a past that has the potential to be inherently destructive to the aims of the colonial project. The 'truth' is therefore deliberately obscured, despite being hidden in plain sight, ensuring Zionism's long-term goals of settler colonial expansion in Palestine remain achievable. This burying of the past operates alongside the Zionist need to foment a new version of the 'truth', as explained by Palestinian academic Walid Khalidi (2005: 43) who argues:

> It was only in 1949, when the Zionists realized that the problem of the Arab refugees was touching the conscience of the civilized world, that they decided to counter the damaging influence it was having on their cause. The story of the Arab evacuation order would hit two birds with one stone. It would absolve the Zionists from the responsibility for the refugees, and it would pin this responsibility on the Arabs themselves.

Against this backdrop of competing historiographies, and in seeking to consider ways of 'revealing' the truth about the past, a burgeoning body of TJ practice has emerged. Amongst the most well-established groups engaged in truth recovery praxis is the Tel Aviv[1] based, Israeli NGO *Zochrot* whose mission statement is to 'promote acknowledgement and accountability for the ongoing injustices of the Palestinian Nakba and to push for the realization of the right of return of the refugees - a precondition for establishing a future Palestinian-Jewish relationship based on justice and equality'. Launched in 2002, the organisations' primary goal has been to (re)educate the Israeli public about the 'truth' surrounding events of 1948, to make the Palestinian narrative around the Nakba more visible and well known, as well as spotlighting the need for a notion of 'justice' that prioritises return or a form of restitution for Palestinian refugees as a precursor to achieving a sustainable peace. To achieve these aims, the organisation developed an oral history platform aimed at collecting testimonies of victims and survivors of the 1948 Nakba, primarily those who became Internally Displaced Persons (IDPs) within the new Israeli State, a process that aligns with many of TJs traditional stated aims around truth recovery in other conflict/transitional contexts. Combining cartography that 'reveals' destroyed Palestinian villages and towns of 1948 alongside digital technology including an 'i-Nakba' app that allows users to visualise original Palestinian villages on their smartphones, *Zochrot* has sought to ensure that the attempted erasure of a Palestinian presence on the land and the subsequent silencing of 'truth'

---

[1] A settlement built on the depopulated Palestinian village of Al-Shaykh Muwannis.

is mitigated. In addition, the organisation has been involved in the facilitation of tours for Israelis and members of the international community to areas where remnants of destroyed Palestinian villages remain. More recently, *Zochrot* have engaged in what would be considered a more conventional approach at truth recovery, mirroring similar practices that have taken place in transitional or post-conflict societies, creating a Truth Commission on the Responsibility of Israeli Society for the Events of 1948–1960 in the Negev, the first of its kind in the region. Owing to its relative success, the work of *Zochrot* has repeatedly been attacked, critiqued, and criminalised. For example, in an article published in *The Times of Israel* (2016), historian Asaf Romirowsky suggested that the group was focused on blaming 'Israel for the Original Sin of its own creation and ostensibly sole responsibility for the Palestinian refugees'.[2] In the same news outlet, Paul Leslie has gone even further to suggest that:

> Promoting false "Nakba-centred" narratives, Zochrot's fabrications suppress the all-important historical context where the inhabitants of the newly independent state were fighting to survive against the well-armed invading armies of several Arab countries, ignore the significant proportion of Israel's population killed during this war and, in several cases, have been shown to distort and falsify the "facts" it communicates about certain Palestinian Arab villages claimed to have been destroyed or abandoned during the fighting.[3]

Beyond simply stating that 'justice' is premised on more than a formal acknowledgement of harm suffered, it is stated on their website that the group endorse the view that 'peace' will only come 'after the country has been decolonized'. However, despite this welcome acknowledgement, academic critique has emerged which has challenged the appropriateness of an Israeli-led organisation spearheading such truth recovery work in this context (Broadhead, 2020; Lentin, 2013; Orr & Golan, 2014). For some, when it comes to the presentation of Palestinian suffering, both historical and present day, there are questions to be raised concerning narrative appropriation, particularly when it relates to the oppression of

---

[2] https://blogs.timesofisrael.com/what-is-zochrot-really-remembering/.

[3] https://blogs.timesofisrael.com/zochrot-the-israeli-equivalent-of-dieudonne-and-his-supporters-updated/.

the Palestinians as a tool for expressing Israeli dissent (Lentin, 2013). Such an intervention is important in that it links to the original steering questions offered by Broadhead (2020) at the beginning of the chapter, in which she challenged those invested in TJ linked to truth recovery in Palestine to consider whether or not there is a role for settlers (broadly defined) when it comes to curating and platforming Palestinian narratives of suffering, particularly when acts of Zionist settler colonial erasure remain ongoing. Furthermore, when considering the appropriateness of this type of truth recovery work being led by Israeli organisations such as *Zochrot*, the words of Edward Said (1984: 34) ring particularly true: 'Facts do not at all speak for themselves, but require a socially acceptable narrative to absorb, sustain and circulate them'. Thus, and in borrowing from the work of Hawari et al. (2019: 162), TJ work related to truth recovery in settler colonial contexts, if it is to be meaningful beyond optics, must involve a process of 'de-normalising and rejecting the production of settler knowledge' in order to ensure that the space exists to produce 'alternative knowledge that can support and sustain a decolonised future'.

Permission to Narrate—Curating the 'Truth' Around Palestinian Loss

On the 22nd of January 2022, Israel's leading 'liberal' newspaper *Haaretz* published an article on the massacre at al-Tantura, a relatively small Palestinian village located on the Mediterranean coast, not far from the city of Haifa. The village had all but been destroyed in 1948 with subsequent claims made by Palestinian witnesses who spoke of massacres committed by the 33rd Battalion of the Zionist Alexandroni Brigade. The article in *Haaretz* documented the location of mass graves existing alongside Israeli leisure facilities and noted 'new' evidence that had been gathered from former Israeli soldiers who, in an apparent crisis of conscience, testified as to what exactly had occurred at the time, including the orders they had been given. However, *Haaretz's* revelation was not revelatory at all. What had been reported had been long acknowledged as the 'truth' by many whose work has documented instances of Zionist settler colonial violence underpinning the formation of the Israeli state-building project in 1948. In fact, Teddy Katz, a former MA student studying under the supervision of Prof. Ilan Pappé, exposed the massacre at al-Tantura sometime before. Writing in a social media post, Pappé noted that, at the time that

Katz's research was made public, the findings were dismissed out of hand, including by *Haaretz* who accused Pappé himself of being 'unprofessional' and a 'lunatic'. In the immediate aftermath of the *Haaretz* report, the PA called for an international investigation into the events that had been reported with several pearl clutching follow-up articles published in local Israeli and international media outlets, reiterating the fact that what transpired at al-Tantura was, surprise surprise, not an isolated incident.

However, by far the most interesting critique, and one that tackled head on the issue of truth recovery that takes place in the context of ongoing settler colonial violence, came from Hashem Abushama (2022). Writing for the Institute of Palestine Studies, Abushama astutely argued that, when it comes to these purported moments of revelation, 'The debates… tell us more about Israeli historiography than they do about the massacred Palestinians. They are reflective of the wider settler colonial power relations that determine *who* remembers, *how* they remember, and according to *whose* archives'. Abushama's intervention speaks perfectly to the words of Said (1984) detailed above and demonstrates how the disclosure of historical 'truths' against the backdrop of ongoing settler colonialism remains a process that is carefully managed and curated, not only by the state itself, but in this instance, emanations of the state, such as its leading print media broadsheet. 'Truths' about Israeli state digressions (read war crimes) can be revealed to the broader Israeli public, including by those outlets that have a purported liberal slant, in such a way as to be careful, sensitive, and regulated, this being the 'major project of Liberal Zionism' (Pappé, 2021). Historical revelations are transformed into palatable 'truths' and are stage managed so as to mitigate against criticism that is too overt, too damning, and therefore detrimental to the overarching aims of the liberal Zionist project. Pappé (2021) continues:

> Liberal Zionism has always been obsessed with finding the balance between the high moral ground and the wish to portray Israel as a civilized State that errs here and there (which usually means killing Palestinians throughout history). The message is clear: none of these mistakes, even if they are war crimes or crimes against humanity, to which the Liberal Zionist admits, should cast doubt on Zionism, or the very idea about the legitimacy of Israel to remain a racist and ethnic Jewish State at the heart of the Arab world.

In a much the same vein, and in reflecting on the recent release of a documentary film entitled 'Schoolyard' that focuses on Israel's bloody assault on Lebanon in 1982 (a campaign that remains a divisive moment in the Israeli state's recent past), historian Seth Anziska points to the growing trend for Israeli soldiers to divulge on camera the truth behind their involvement in historical violent actions. Anziska suggests that the willingness to brazenly admit to involvement in alleged war crimes, either in Tantura or in South Lebanon, in front of a camera, is revelatory in that it demonstrates the extent to which Israeli impunity and a lack of accountability have become ingrained:

> In this 21st century Israeli landscape, the documentary may be politically extraneous, but it is a mirror to shifting societal norms, of a moral universe moving from angst and fear of persecution toward a willingness to disclose past indiscretions, even with pride. The need to speak of war crimes suggests a particular form of guilt and a warped memorialization practice that is taking shape.

Such instances of Israeli impunity are hardly consigned to history. Linking the testimonies in 'Schoolyard' to the rehabilitation of Elor Azaria—the Israeli soldier who shot dead an incapacitated Palestinian in Hebron in 2016—is a clever way of demonstrating the extent to which a lack of accountability for grievous breaches of International Humanitarian Law (IHL) is an all pervasive and embedded feature of Israeli society. Outright refusal to prosecute is set alongside the deliberate obfuscation of the 'truth' surrounding what are indisputable facts, such as those which have been shown to be the case in the murder of prominent Palestinian reporter, Shireen Abu Akleh, shot dead whilst on mission in the Palestinian city of Jenin. Anziska further argues: 'Abu Akleh's death… illustrates one fundamental lesson of 1982: that without redress for historic and ongoing war crimes, Israeli society will remain in the throes of violence, stripped of hindsight, unable to confront the consequences of individual or state action'. What all of this demonstrates, I suggest, is that when it comes to implementation of TJ practices involved in truth recovery, specifically when they are trialled in areas where settler colonial erasure of the Indigenous population remains a guiding principle of the colonial power, the central concern must be on issues relating to: who gets to speak; who has permission to narrate; who is afforded a platform; and how 'truths' about the past are revealed. This, I suggest, is as important, if not more so, than the very act of truth recovery itself. In addition, the revelation of historical truths cannot be seen as a substitute for pursuing 'justice'. 'Even the worst atrocity can be tolerated and explained' as Pappé (2021) has suggested, and as a result, 'the discreet dots of Israeli criminality are not connected together to provide the full and truthful picture of the real intent of the settler- colonial project of Zionism'.

Conclusion

Truth recovery practices that take place against the backdrop of ongoing attempts at Indigenous erasure must seek to 'narrate new counter-hegemonic narratives and devise fresh liberationist and decolonising strategies' (Masalha, 2012: 256) if they are to meaningfully disrupt and agitate the liberal status quo. Revelation without recourse to repair serves no useful purpose and runs the risk of allowing for a sense of closure, dislocating the violence of the past from the ongoing colonial violence of the present day—akin to a metaphorical drawing of a line in the sand. Therefore, when pursuing truth recovery as a mode of TJ praxis in Palestine-Israel, those actors who do so must retain a steadfast commitment to a decolonial praxis that reverses and repairs the damage done, and in so doing, they must seek to disrupt an 'orthodox transitional justice paradigm' (Park, 2020: 265). This process of challenging collective state-sponsored amnesia is hard, as has been noted above, and is 'a workaday exercise, involving academic controversy, political debate, media revelations, processes of proof and disproof. Even where individual perpetrators of past abuse deny or suppress individual memory of it, these processes of public debate are likely to result in exposure' (Asmal et al., 1997: 10).

In sites of ongoing settler colonial violence, greater scrutiny must also be placed on who it is that is assuming the lead role when uncovering past historical truths. Sitting with uncomfortable truths about the past, in any settler colonial context, requires, and ultimately benefits from, the active involvement of the 'settler' community. However, the involvement of the settler community cannot be done in such a way as to allow for the assuaging of feelings of collective guilt or to seek pardon without a commitment to action. Revelations about the violence of the past must be linked to ways of actively disrupting and unravelling the foundations of the Zionist settler colonial project in historic Palestine and must do so by reconstructing and reclaiming the historical realities that underpin

Palestinian loss and erasure, not only in 1948, but before and ever since. Rebuilding Palestine cannot be based on the parameters set by the failed peacebuilding model, nor can it reinforce the mould of a two-state solution, one that embeds inequitable partition, a process that has long since been revealed as dead in the water and which was (and is) premised on Palestinian concession. Moreover, if revelations of the past are not linked to demands for repair, this form of truth recovery praxis is an exercise in academic navel gazing and must be turned away from. As Roberts (2020) has advanced, if detached from the advancement of meaningful action around undoing years of structural inequality, truth recovery processes serve the function of being a liberalising force more focused on assuaging settler guilt than engaging with the legitimate demands of decolonisation for a long-suffering people. In this context, decolonial conversations must be led by Palestinians, those who bear the brunt of ongoing processes of colonial exploitation and must include the many disparate voices of the Palestinian populace, including those who live in the West Bank, the Gaza Strip, within 1948 Israel and across the wider diaspora. The exclusion of any constituent element of the Palestinian people would render conversations around truth and the subsequent demand for repair, as partial and limited, amounting to an extension of the liberal peacebuilding paradigm.

References

Abushama, H. (2022). *'According to whose archives?': The Tantura massacre and revisionist Israeli historiography*. Institute for Palestine Studies. https://www.palestine-studies.org/en/node/1652421

Amara, A., & Hawari, Y. (2019). *Using indigeneity in the struggle for Palestinian liberation*. https://al-shabaka.org/commentaries/using-indigeneity-in-the-struggle-for-palestinian-liberation/

Anziska, S. (2019). Special document file: The erasure of the Nakba in Israel's archives. *Journal of Palestine Studies, 49*(1), 64–76.

Anziska, S. (2022). Confession without consequence (972mag.com). https://www.972mag.com/schoolyard-film-lebanon-israel-nakba/ Accessed 10th October 2022.

Asmal, K., Asmal, L., & Roberts, R. S. (1997). *Reconciliation through truth: A reckoning of apartheid's criminal governance* (No. 74). New Africa Books.

Baconi, T. (2022). *Critique as movement building: The apartheid reports on Palestine*. https://www.madamasr.com/en/2022/03/29/opinion/u/critique-as-movement-building-the-apartheid-reports-on-palestine/

Bracka, J. M. (2017). "From banning Nakba to bridging narratives": the collective memory of 1948 and transitional justice for Israelis and Palestinians. In *Law and Memory: Towards Legal Governance of History* (pp. 348–373). Cambridge University Press.

Broadhead, L. (2020). Scales of justice: Putting remembrance back on the map in Palestine and Mi'kma'ki. *Settler Colonial Studies, 10*(3), 331–352.

Browne, B. C. (2017). Transitional justice and the case of Palestine. In C. Lawther, L. Moffett, & D. Jacobs (Eds.), *Research handbook on transitional justice*. Edward Elgar.

Browne, B. C. (2021). Disrupting settler-colonialism or enforcing the liberal "peace"? Transitional (in)justice in Palestine-Israel. *Journal of Holy Land and Palestine Studies, 20*(1), 1–27. https://doi.org/10.3366/hlps.2021.0255

Butler, J. (2006). *Precarious life*. Nueva York.

Hawari, Y., Plonski, S., & Weizman, E. (2019). Seeing Israel through Palestine: Knowledge production as anti-colonial praxis. *Settler Colonial Studies, 9*(1), 155–175.

Hayner, P. B. (2002). *Unspeakable truths: Confronting state terror and atrocity*. Routledge.

Jamar, A. (2019). *The crusade of transitional justice tracing the journeys of hegemonic claims in violence and democracy*. The British Academy.

Josh Ruebner. (2022). 'Five things the United States knew about the Nakba as it unfolded' | Middle East Institute (mei.edu). Accessed 14th November 2022.

Karsh, E. (2010). *Palestine betrayed*. Yale University Press.

Khalidi, W. (2005). Why did the Palestinians leave, revisited. *Journal of Palestine Studies, 34*(2), 42–54.

Khoury, N. (2016). National narratives and the Oslo peace process: How peace-building paradigms address conflicts over history. *Nations and Nationalism, 22*(3), 465–483.

Lentin, R. (2013). *Co-memory and melancholia: Memorialising the Palestinian Nakba*. Manchester University Press.

Masalha, N. (2012). *The Palestine Nakba: Decolonising history, narrating the subaltern, reclaiming memory*. Zed Books.

Nagy, R. (2022). Transformative justice in a settler colonial transition: Implementing the UN Declaration on the rights of indigenous peoples in Canada. *The International Journal of Human Rights, 26*(2), 191–216.

Orr, Z., & Golan, D. (2014). Human rights NGOs in Israel: Collective memory and denial. *The International Journal of Human Rights, 18*(1), 68–93.

Pappé, I. (2007). *The ethnic cleansing of Palestine*. Simon and Schuster.

Pappé, I. (2018). *Finding the truth amid Israel's lies*. Electronic Intifada. https://electronicintifada.net/content/finding-truth-amid-israels-lies/24531

Pappé, I. (2020). An indicative archive: Salvaging Nakba documents. *Journal of Palestine Studies, 49*(3), 22–40.

Pappé, I. (2021). *On Haaretz: Can settler colonialism be liberal and apartheid be progressive?* The Palestine Chronicle. https://www.palestinechronicle.com/on-haaretz-can-settler-colonialism-be-liberal-and-apartheid-be-progressive/

Park, A. S. J. (2015). Settler colonialism and the politics of grief: Theorising a decolonising transitional justice for Indian residential schools. *Human Rights Review, 16*(3), 273–293. https://doi.org/10.1007/s12142-015-0372-4

Park, A. S. J. (2020). Settler colonialism, decolonization and radicalizing transitional justice. *International Journal of Transitional Justice, 14*(2), 260–279. https://doi.org/10.1093/ijtj/ijaa006

Roberts, R. S. (2020). How "transitional justice" colonized South Africa's TRC. *Modern Languages Open* (1). https://doi.org/10.3828/mlo.v0i0.318

Said, E. (1984). Permission to narrate. *Journal of Palestine Studies, 13*(3), 27–48. https://doi.org/10.2307/2536688

Shalhoub-Kevorkian, N. (2015). *Security theology, surveillance and the politics of fear*. Cambridge University Press.

Smyth, M. B. (2007). *Truth recovery and justice after conflict: Managing violent pasts*. Routledge.

Veracini, L. (2013). 'Settler colonialism': Career of a concept. *The Journal of Imperial and Commonwealth History, 41*(2), 313–333.

Veracini, L. (2014). Understanding colonialism and settler colonialism as distinct formations. *Interventions, 16*(5), 615–633.

Wolfe, P. (2006). Settler colonialism and the elimination of the native. *Journal of Genocide Research, 8*(4), 387–409.

CHAPTER 4

Pursuing International Criminal Justice, the ICC, and Palestine

Abstract The aim here is to trace some of the arguments that have been offered regarding what role (if any) recourse to the ICC might play in the pursuit of a decolonised Palestine. Since 2009, there has been a clear shift within the upper echelons of the Palestinian political elite towards embracing the potentialities of the ICC as a way of spotlighting widespread Israeli state-sponsored human rights abuses through pursuit of prosecutions against individuals representing the Israeli state. Like all persons who have suffered the violent scourge of colonialism, international law has operated against the Palestinians as a method of violation and denial, rather than emancipation and justice; ensuring the maintenance of a permanent state of exception, rather than providing for a legal framework that advances redress and alleviation. Therefore, in following this logic, pursuing elite, top-down interventions will always be in some ways unsatisfactory and can never act as a 'justice' panacea.

Keywords International law · Tribunals · Prosecution · Top-down · Grassroots

> The unpreparedness of the educated classes, the lack of practical links between them and the mass of the people, their laziness, and, let it be

© The Author(s), under exclusive license to Springer Nature Switzerland AG 2023
B. C. Browne, *Transitional (in)Justice and Enforcing the Peace on Palestine*, Rethinking Peace and Conflict Studies,
https://doi.org/10.1007/978-3-031-25394-2_4

said, their cowardice at the decisive moment of the struggle will give rise to tragic mishaps.

Frantz Fanon

INTRODUCTION

The prosecution of those responsible for committing war crimes, including crimes against humanity and genocide, is a central component of TJ, with the pursuit of individual accountability through an internationally sponsored criminal court a common route pursued by newly installed democratic regimes keen to draw a line under the past. As 'the most recognisable of the transitional justice mechanisms' (Panepinto, 2014: 9), International Criminal Justice (ICJ), embodied through the establishment of ad hoc criminal tribunals and a permanent International Criminal Court (ICC) based in the Hague, has come to represent the gold standard when it comes to advancing the cause of post-conflict 'justice'. High-profile tribunals mandated to investigate war crimes in the former Yugoslavia and Rwanda (ICTY/ICTR) and subsequent hybrid tribunals established for Sierra Leone and Cambodia helped to engrain this orthodox viewpoint, providing a blueprint upon which the ICC was established following the ratification of the Rome Statute in 2002. At the time of writing, and according to the institution's homepage, until now there have been:

> 31 cases before the Court, with some cases having more than one suspect. ICC judges have issued 37 arrest warrants… 21 people have been detained in the ICC detention centre and have appeared before the Court. 12 people remain at large. Charges have been dropped against 3 people due to their deaths. ICC judges have also issued 9 summonses to appear. The judges have issued 10 convictions and 4 acquittals.

The evolving nature of modern warfare, evidenced by a proliferation of longer, more protracted intra-state conflicts and a plurality of state and non-state Actors, often results in stalemate and thus no clear transition from an old to a new regime. As a result, ICJ has pivoted to evade the need for an exclusive 'post-conflict' moment in time (Hansen, 2019). Subsequently, the ICC has issued international arrest warrants against those it accuses of war crimes at a time whilst the conflict in question remains ongoing. High-profile instances include the ICCs pursuit of Sudanese former President, Omar Hassan Ahmad Al-Bashir, former senior South Ossetian Minister, David Georgiyevich Sanakoev, and alleged former Lieutenant General of the Libyan army and former head of the Libyan Internal Security Agency (ISA), Tohami Mohamed Khaled. Critics of the operational capacity of the ICC include international lawyers who have a body of scholarly work on Palestine. Azarova and Mariniello (2017) point to the underwhelming performance of the court as being 'symptomatic of its highly-politicised mandate' which in turn, they argue, has compromised 'its institutional integrity, effectiveness and legitimacy'. Notwithstanding the shortcomings, support for this type of intervention remains strong, with many still viewing the pursuit of individualised 'retributive justice as the ideal response to mass impunity' (Bracka, 2021: 324) despite limited evidence to discern efficacy, particularly when it comes to embedding fragile peace processes, or deterring future war crimes, crimes against humanity, and genocide.

A cursory glance at the active and past arrest warrants issued by the Office of the Prosecutor (OTP) is also revelatory (conspicuously absent on the list of arrest warrants are those who bear greatest responsibility for leading illegal wars in Iraq, Libya, and Afghanistan). This I suggest is directly relevant when we consider this form of TJ intervention and the potential role of the court when it comes to choosing whether or not to engage in the situation in Palestine. A number of structural limitations have also been highlighted which give rise to a charge of the institution's selectivity when it comes to deciding which 'conflicts are worth pursuing 'justice' for, and which are not'. The ICCs seemingly disproportionate focus on despotic regimes in the 'Global South' whilst simultaneously eschewing its responsibility to pursue leaders of supposed 'superpowers' allegedly responsible for committing war crimes adds fire to the flames of discontent. Whilst narratives of racism and claims of an anti-African bias have long been advanced in certain circles, including by the African Union (AU)—most recently during the court's pursuit of Kenyan and Sudanese leaders, Uhuru Kenyatta and Omar Al-Bashir—leading TWAIL scholar Mutua (2016: 47) warns against 'buckling to this neo-colonialist charge' pointing to the problematic role of the AU itself when sheltering leaders responsible for committing atrocities, whilst at the same time acknowledging that there are 'structural, normative, and institutional deficits' hindering the court's performance. Mutua (2016) instead challenges the court to 'tackle questions of hegemonic disequilibria' if it is to seek to become an effective institution. For those invested in the cause of 'justice' in Palestine and who see possibilities through engagement with the ICC, the issues around operational disequilibria, more specifically the potential for selectivity in terms of the pursuit of 'justice', should serve as a warning.

The aim here is to trace some of the arguments that have been offered regarding what role (if any) recourse to the ICC might play in the pursuit of a decolonised Palestine. Since 2009, there has been a clear shift within the upper echelons of the Palestinian political elite towards embracing the potentialities of the ICC as a way of challenging widespread Israeli state-sponsored human rights abuses through pursuit of prosecutions against individuals representing the Israeli state. When it first opened its preliminary examination into Palestine in 2015, the decision to do so was met with optimism, labelled as a 'turning point' and 'game changing' (Bracka, 2021: 285). However, rather than being seen as a move to chase 'justice', embracing the possibilities attached to engagement with the ICC has been interpreted by many critical legal scholars on Palestine as a way for the PA to gain political leverage and to advance its statist aspirations. In doing so, it is hoped that the grossly asymmetrical power imbalance that characterises the relationship between coloniser and colonised can further be illuminated and the deep seeded hypocrisy of the West in terms of its unyielding support of the Zionist settler colonial project be exposed. This form of engagement with the ICC can thus be interpreted as an opportunity to embarrass, rather than holding to account, the Israeli state, and when we consider the ongoing and steady attempts at erasure of the Indigenous Palestinian population, the need to do so could hardly be more pressing. As such, one must therefore always tread carefully before pouring cold water on such pragmatism when alternative solutions are in short supply. In more recent years, alongside Palestinian political endorsement, leading NGOs working in and on Palestine have been invited to submit amicus curiae briefs to the OTP relating to the situation on the ground. High-profile human rights and civil society organisations including: the Palestinian Centre for Human Rights, Al Haq, Al Mezan, Bt'selem, and Adalah have all presented caches of evidence of alleged Israeli war crimes. The invitation to do so comes against the backdrop of a long and protracted dispute over issues relating to the court's jurisdiction relating to Palestine's legal status.

The fraught history of international law and its (mis)application against the Palestinian people generates understandable scepticism, including amongst established and internationally acclaimed legal experts with a lifetime and body of work pressed in service of Palestinian liberation. Like all persons who have suffered the violent scourge of colonialism, international law has operated against the Palestinians as a method of violation and denial, rather than emancipation and justice; ensuring the maintenance of a permanent state of exception, rather than providing for a legal framework that advances redress and alleviation. Therefore, in following this logic, pursuing elite, top-down interventions will always be in some ways unsatisfactory and can never act as a 'justice' panacea. Conversely, the pursuit of top-down retributive justice may in fact lead to a further marginalisation of the ultimate goal of Palestinian decolonisation by allowing for a few high-profile cases to be considered in isolation. Whilst there have been a number of important legal interventions on the situation in Palestine, including Advisory Opinions from the International Court of Justice and condemnatory statements made by the United Nations General Assembly, a lack of political will to ensure judicial enforceability reveals the limitations within the existing regulatory framework towards vigorously holding the Israeli state accountable. In the absence of tangible evidence to suggest that ICJ can aid in the generation of a decolonial post-conflict reality in Palestine or help shift the conflict dynamic 'on the ground', providing a discernible pathway to peace that is justice anchored, minimifidianism surrounding this form of 'top-down' TJ intervention abounds. As such, when one views the ICCs engagement in Palestine/Israel alongside the myriad examples of other international law intrusions to date, what is clear is that 'justice' for Palestine and the Palestinians will never solely be gleaned from within the outworking of international legal frameworks, a point long since made by almost every critical Palestinian lawyer. Similarly, in noting that there exists no 'legal or political pathway to decolonisation' (Halper, 2021: 125) the limitations of pursuing top-down interventions ought to be more carefully considered.

In critiquing the purported strengths and limitations of this form of TJ, an extensive body of academic work has provided the intellectual scaffolding, including, *inter alia*, Erakat (2019), Imseis (2020), Falk (2017), Azarova and Mariniello (2017), Bisharat et al. (2018), Kearney and Reynolds (2013), Dugard and Reynolds (2013), Cavanaugh (2002), and Hansen (2019). Here, the argument is made that in embracing the ICC, the aim for the Palestinian political establishment, one that is well past its sell buy date, is about securing political clout, chasing a nationalist/two-state dream and advancing the 'legitimacy war' rather than vigorously aiming for meaningful 'justice', one based on a decolonial framework that safeguards reparations and demands implementation of the sacrosanct right of return. Recourse through the apparatus of the ICC, if done in isolation, has the potential to allow for the individualisation of culpability, the side-lining of broader structural concerns, and arguably reduces overall scrutiny on Israel's role as a settler colonial entity. More concerningly, any wholehearted engagement with the ICC by the Palestinian political leadership runs the risk of setting Palestinian anti-colonial resistance alongside Israeli state-sponsored violence (Halper, 2021). Therefore, if it is to play a supportive role in advancing 'justice' demands in Palestine, engagement with the ICC must be viewed as a strategy that compliments, not deters, other modes of resistance, including grassroots justice interventions, in order to yield the best possible outcome. Steering questions to be considered throughout this chapter include: to what extent is it politically expedient or naïve to pursue recourse before the ICC when one considers the violent legacy of international law on Palestine and the Palestinians? Next, if the argument proposed is that engagement with the ICC can help to advance the 'legitimacy war' against Israel, what happens when the ICC begins to target Palestinian resistance (however conceived) equating it alongside Israeli state-sponsored violence? Moreover, and drawing on the legitimate concerns raised by Halper (2021: 123) if international criminal law is the supreme example of 'Big power' hegemony hiding behind liberal forms of governmentality, to what extent will Palestinian claims for 'justice' ever receive a fair hearing? And, most pressingly, given that legal routes towards realising meaningful decolonisation in Palestine are presently non-existent, can engagement in international criminal law ever meaningfully be pivoted in order to help reach this desired outcome?

INTERNATIONAL LAW, THE ICC, AND PALESTINE

'Very few conflicts' as Noura Erakat (2019: 3) notes 'have been as defined by astute attention to law and legal controversy as this one'. As a useful tool at the disposal of the Israeli state, international law has been selectively deployed and creatively interpreted in such a way as to ensure that the hegemonic and privileged status of the settler colonial power is maintained at the expense of the Indigenous Palestinian population, aided and abetted by both the active and passive support of the west. In interpreting the legal foundations that undergird the formation of the Israeli state,

Nicola Perugini and Neve Gordon (2015: 34) point to 'The framing of Israel's establishment as a humanitarian solution' which they argue 'provided its settler colonial nature with an aura of international legitimacy'. Since the start of the British Mandate in 1922, 'Palestinians have literally fought against their state of exception' with Israel using 'its military and economic power, as well as its alliances to global superpowers in the past and present, to advance its claims so that it can create alternative legal models for regulating Palestinian life' (Erakat, 2019: 17). Bisharat et al. (2018: 1) further note that 'Due to Israel's disregard for international law and privileged treatment by powerful countries unconcerned by its repeated violations of human rights, international law has understandably been regarded with a high level of scepticism by many Palestinians'. When we recall that the catastrophic fragmentation and destruction of historic Palestine was a process that was initiated and facilitated under the auspices of international law, proposed by the United Nations against the will of the Palestinian population, and imposed through a combination of aid and support to the fledgling Israeli state, propped up with military force, such scepticism is hardly surprising. It can be argued then that the language of international law has been and continues to be selectively applied and eschewed in equal measure and as a result, has been successful in marginalising a decolonial and 'justice'-focused reality in and for Palestine and the Palestinians. The aim for Palestinian lawyers and international allies ever since has been to critique and challenge the misapplication of international law, by exposing its flaws, limitations, and ingrained hypocrisy, in an effort to support political strategies to mitigate this exceptionalism. Or, as Erakat (2019: 4) has argued, to examine the way it has been weaponised against Palestinians up until now so as to attempt to have it 'wielded in the sophisticated service of a political movement'. Erakat (2019: 6) continues:

> It is this indeterminacy in law and its utility as a means to dominate as well as to fight that makes it at once a site of oppression and of resistance, at once a source of legitimacy and a legitimating veneer of bare violence, and at once the target of protest and a tool for protest.

At the grassroots level, Palestinian advocacy has long been involved in creatively and resolutely ensuring that the myriad justice issues that impact the everyday lives of Palestinians remain in focus and are framed within the wider context of attempts at ongoing settler colonial erasure.

Creatively engaging in this form of 'lawfare', it is argued, can help to overcome Palestinian exceptionalism (Falk, 2017). However, the pursuit of retributive justice through recourse to the ICC is a strategy spearheaded primarily by the Palestinian political elite (albeit with more recent local NGO buy in). International law has long been used as a policy instrument when managing inter-state relationships and when seeking to resolve disputes (Falk, 2017). Pursuit of this formal top-down TJ linked to criminal accountability for international crimes can be interpreted as a creative way of pivoting existing legal frameworks, which in turn can help to expand legal definitions and parameters in such a way as to help to engage with the myriad enduring 'justice' issues that remain central to the 'conflict' (Erakat, 2019; Imseis, 2020). However, rather than being about the pursuit of justice, in appealing to the ICC the goal of the PA is to maintain political pressure on the Israeli state, with a view to winning the 'legitimacy war' in the eyes of an increasingly sympathetic international audience. The growing global interest in the case of Palestine before the ICC is due, in many ways to the fact that for the overwhelming number of states who make up the United Nations General Assembly (UNGA) 'The Palestinian situation… constitutes a struggle by its people for self-determination in a period regarded as post-colonial, against a state which has the support of the world's last remaining superpower and which invokes a moral rationale based on the long history of oppression suffered by the Jewish people' (Turner, 2015: 155). However, Palestine's road towards the ICC, however, 'is marked by missed opportunities from the perspective of the court's role and its fraught mandate of attempting to contribute to peace making' (Azarova & Mariniello, 2017).

Despite having initially ratified the Rome Statute which gave rise to the formation of the ICC, Israel's support has long since been withdrawn and its stance over the past number of years has been to refute the court's jurisdictional claims over cases in the Occupied Territories. As a result, the PA's move towards the ICC has drawn predictable criticism from Israel and its closest ally, the United States, who accuse the Palestinian leadership of choosing a path that undermines the cause of 'peace'. Unilateral initiatives that attempt to place blame on one side, or so the argument goes, undermine the spirit of the (outdated and inherently flawed) Oslo Accords. Yet, in embracing the ICC, the Palestinians have publicly declared their open expression of 'no confidence in further negotiations carried on within the Oslo framework' (Falk, 2017: 91). Whilst the goal of the ICC, as an institution, is to combat impunity and ensure that crimes that 'deeply shock the conscience of humanity' are tried in an international setting, Azarova (2015) notes that 'Regrettably, all sides have subjected Palestine's move to trigger ICC jurisdiction – and with it, the basic service of justice – to the politics and compromises of the Palestinian statehood bid'. The move by the Palestinian leadership to initiate proceedings before the ICC came amidst a flurry of accusations of Israeli breaches of international law, including alleged war crimes committed during operation 'Cast Lead', the late December (2008) genocidal assault on the Gaza Strip which resulted in the death of over 1400 Palestinians (mostly civilians) and the widespread and wanton destruction of the fabric of Palestinian society (Adem, 2019). Findings of alleged war crimes and breaches of international law were reaffirmed by a number of legal bodies, including in a UN report led by Richard Goldstone which placed the blame on both sides, accusing both Israel and the Palestinian faction Hamas.

The subsequent request to begin a preliminary examination of crimes committed on the territory of Palestine was initiated on the 22nd of January 2009 by spokesperson for the Government of Palestine, Minister of Justice, Mr Ali Khashan, pursuant to the terms listed in Article 12(3) of the Rome Statute. The referral sparked a period of legal consternation, with those keen on stalling the process of accession making arguments pertaining to Palestine's legal status (or lack thereof) at the UN. This question of ICC jurisdiction to investigate alleged crimes on the Palestinian Territories was intricately linked to the issue of Palestinian statehood, and thus, whereas justice for victims and survivors of the 2008 Gaza War was emphasised as a priority for the Palestinian leadership, the move can be interpreted as a supreme engagement in high political brinkmanship—an attempt towards advancing Palestine's claim for statehood with the attendant international recognition that such a bid would bring. Any recognition of the jurisdiction of the ICC could ultimately result in international pressure being brought to bear on the Israeli government, one that had shown little interest in agreeing to be bound by previous internationally sponsored 'peace' accords. In reaffirming jurisdiction, the ICC could help to cement notions of Palestinian statehood and thus prop up the infrastructure and apparatus of the PA.

The various hurdles that had to be overcome before Palestine's application for membership of the ICC came into force on 1st April 2015 are, I suggest, symptomatic of Palestine's treatment under international law more broadly up until this point. Following over three years of deliberation, in 2012 the then Prosecutor, Luis Moreno Ocampo declared Palestine's uncertain legal status at the UN a bar to initiating proceedings before the ICC. Despite appearing to be a setback of sorts, the Prosecutor deferred to the UNGA, an organ that had been more receptive to Palestinian statehood, the question of jurisdiction and Palestine's status as a state (on the basis that successful accession to the ICC could be attained in the future should the issue of statehood be ironed out). The result was Palestinian President, Mahmoud Abbas, appearing before the UNGA filing an official submission to become recognised as the 194th member of the UN (a decision subsequently endorsed by 138 votes to nine, with 41 choosing to abstain). On the 29th of November 2012, Palestine was granted 'non-member observer State status in the United Nations' under UN Resolution 67/19. Far from being about pursuing justice for victims and survivors, the Palestinian leadership's move towards ICC membership followed a pattern of stately like behaviour, from gaining membership to other UN organisations (such as UNESCO in 2011) to endorsing prominent international legal treaties (Azarova, 2015). Most recently, and following a call from the OTP, between January and March 2020, '43 amicus briefs had been submitted to the Pre-Trial Chamber of the International Criminal Court on the Situation in Palestine, among them an unprecedented number of briefs... filed by states' (Kearney, 2020). Whilst this interest in Palestine before the ICC is significant, it would be naive to suggest this to be some form of moral reckoning by an international community shamed into action. The briefs submitted to the Pre-Trial Chamber of the ICC included those drafted by several European states including Germany, who called into question the very appropriateness of the court in choosing to engage with the case in the first place. In addition, there were several states who called on the Palestinian leadership to avoid pursuing action before the ICC as it had the potential to damage further 'peace negotiations' with Israel, returning to the language of 'liberal peacebuilding' and reinforcing the primacy of the Accords.

Israel's response to the Palestinian application to the ICC throughout the process has been to bluntly refuse to cooperate with any investigation, as evidenced when a channel of dialogue was opened up by the Israeli government with the OTP with the sole purpose of explaining the ICCs' lack of jurisdiction rather than accepting the Court's mandate to investigate alleged crimes committed by Israeli forces during their attack on the Gaza Strip in 2014 code named 'Operation Protective Edge'. Israel's rejection of the ICC, notably an institution borne out of a desire to ensure retributive justice is meted out for crimes that share similarities to those unearthed during the International Military Tribunals established at Nuremberg to try leading Nazis, is according to Reynolds (2016) absurd and completely logical in equal measure. The legal foundations upon which the Rome Statute is built are solid and have been endorsed by over 124 states, and its very existence does little to challenge the sovereignty of any state, including Israel. However, as Reynolds (2016) suggests, the rejection of the court's jurisdiction and the subsequent refusal to engage with investigative procedures is perfectly logical when one acknowledges that 'Israeli officials stand to lose a great deal from any formal probe into their conduct and ongoing domination of occupied Palestinian territory'. According to Osiel (2015: 13), the Palestinian decision to engage with this form of top-down TJ represents a change in mindset within the leadership—from heroic and triumphant anti-colonialists to advancing 'a humanitarian narrative, of tragic personal victimhood and hopelessness, of immobilizing passivity under the continuous onslaught of human rights violations and systematic war crime'. Falk (2017: 89) further notes that such moves towards 'legal remedies in international law' can be viewed as a 'preferred alternative to either "armed struggle" or a failed diplomacy'. For the purposes of this chapter, when we consider the manner in which international law has operated against the Palestinians to date—acting in such a way as to exclude rather than supporting Palestine's pursuit of a decolonial 'justice'—this move towards the ICC, I suggest, has the potential to add layers of bureaucracy, rather than squash the deep asymmetries that exist between coloniser and colonised, and, more pressingly may result in a sharpening of criticism around Palestinian anti-colonial resistance. Thus, ultimately when it pertains to engagement in this form of top-down TJ intervention, it could be argued that the Palestinians have as much to lose as their occupier.

THERE IS NO JUSTICE TO BE GLEANED FROM INTERNATIONAL LAW

In considering its failure to stymie Zionist settler colonial expansion in Palestine, Abunimah (2006) points to a long history of flawed international law interventions. Referencing specifically the much lauded ICJ ruling on 'The Wall', Abunimah (2006: 35) notes that, almost twenty-five years prior, the UN Security Council (in Resolution 465 [1980]) passed judgement on the illegality of the situation on the ground, highlighting that 'all measures taken by Israel to change the physical character, demographic composition, institutional structure, or status of the Palestinian and other Arab territories occupied since 1967, including Jerusalem, or any part thereof, have no legal validity and that Israel's policy and practices of settling parts of its population and new immigrants in those territories constitute a flagrant violation of the Fourth Geneva Convention relative to the Protection of Civilian Persons in Time of War'. Thus, criticism of Israeli crimes against the Indigenous Palestinian population and violations of international law are long-standing, all of which further reveals that 'International law is simply powerless unless the political will exists to enforce it by compelling an offending country to comply' (Abunimah, 2006: 37). Public condemnations, whilst notable, serve only to sharpen the sense of Palestinian exceptionalism when they are met with inaction in holding the Israeli state accountable, and far from bringing pressure to bear, if anything, the material reality on the ground has become markedly worse. More pertinently, when it comes to the problematic role of liberal peacebuilding interventions in Palestine, the judgements and condemnations issued by international organs and endorsed by international stakeholders to the 'conflict' are fundamentally flawed in that they are undergirded by the repeated insistence that any resolution to the 'conflict' resides in the language enshrined within the existing Oslo Accords.

In drawing attention to this specific issue, Imseis (2020: 16) considers one of the main stumbling blocks in pivoting international law in service of the Palestinian cause to be 'The UN's handling of Israel's prolonged occupation of the OPT', which has failed to 'definitively determine that presence to be illegal on the basis of its own UN record and has made its end subject to negotiation'. International law and those organs who act as arbiters for the management of inter-state conflict continue to set limitations and to define the parameters around what any future decolonial reality will look like in Palestine, returning, as always, to the original sin of partition in 1948 as the basis for negotiation without sufficiently providing for meaningful recompense for the subsequent destruction of the land, and forced exile of the Indigenous population. This return to 1948 as the basis and starting point for any future negotiations between the Palestinians and the Israelis is even more significant according to Halper (2021: 126) in that it highlights the lack of willingness on behalf of the international community to even consider the legitimate anticolonial demands of those Palestinians living in Israel or those who live in forced exile in the wider diaspora. Despite a recent UNGA (Fourth committee) vote in favour of a second advisory opinion investigating Israel's 'prolonged occupation, settlement and annexation of Palestinian territory'—a decision that was met with opprobrium by Israeli political leaders—the parameters and potential scope of the investigation remain limited. Thus, if we accept that this is the way international law has operated, and continues to operate in the region, acting to exclude rather than empower Palestinians, what merit is there in appealing to the ICC, this supreme example of top-down TJ?

The Palestinian leadership's courting of the ICC makes sense in that it permits the guise of being seen to be operating as one would expect a normal state to act; it allows the leadership to appear to be acting in pursuit of 'justice' for the Palestinian population whilst simultaneously retaining the established legal order, reaffirming a commitment to the primacy of international law (despite its imperialist and exceptionalist underpinnings), propping up the Oslo Process that maintains its own legitimacy. Thus, the hegemonic (and problematic) status quo remains untouched. This purported limitation in pursuing 'justice' through appealing to the ICC chimes with similar sentiments from Mezna Qato and Kareem Rabie (2013) who caution against framing the pursuit of Palestinian liberation squarely within the language of international law. Whilst their critique is not directed at the ICC specifically, the authors spotlight similar arguments on how international law contains, rather than providing emancipatory opportunities. When it comes to pivoting international law in pursuit of Palestinian liberation, they note:

> Almost all prominent Palestine organising, including the solidarity movement, bases the struggle and its claims on international law... We support BDS as a potentially fluid and inclusive solidarity tactic, but we consider it problematic to pivot movement strategy on bodies of law that emerged in order to regulate imperialism, and that often function to legalize Israeli colonisation and colonialism.

To be sure, the authors accept that the vocal critics of international law, particularly within the Palestinian legal community, have greatly advanced our understanding of its imperialist underpinnings and have long pointed to its inherent limitations when being pressed into service for decolonial justice in Palestine. However, the authors advance a compelling argument that the framing of international law 'has transformed liberal, left, and Palestine solidarity discourse into a question of rights' to the detriment of advancing more meaningful conversations around how best to achieve a decolonial future. In following this logic, it can reasonably be argued then that the pursuit of top-down ICJ intervention, including for the purposes of this chapter appealing to the ICC, is a strategy that is inherently flawed and potentially self-defeating. They continue:

> The controversy over the utility of the law is as well known in Palestine as it is elsewhere: international judicial rulings against the separation wall may move it a few meters, but they don't challenge its existence, or the occupation that put it there. There is a real question about what specifically the law can ameliorate for Palestinians under occupation and in diaspora, but there is also a larger issue. The move towards legal practice was supposed to step around the bogus peace process, and to get us beyond the logic of negotiations. Legal rulings can lead to small changes in their status on the ground, or big changes in the UN, but the West Bank and Gaza remain in a state of suspension within Israeli colonial logics.

Dissenters of the ICC, and of ICJ more generally, have long pointed to its blindness when it comes to addressing broader structural concerns in any active conflict due primarily to the fact that it remains embedded in a 'liberal, colonialist or gendered legal paradigm' (McAuliffe & Schwöbel-Patel, 2018: 990). Similar critiques have been offered by scholars versed in the Third World Approaches to International Law (TWAIL) tradition, and who have provided an extensive volume of work that points to its colonial underpinnings, as deriving from a 'predatory system that legitimizes, reproduces, and sustains the plunder and subordination of the Third World by the West' (Mutua, 2000). The pursuit of individual criminal responsibility through recourse to ICJ, according to McAuliffe and Schwöbel-Patel (2018: 1001), 'fails to properly situate crimes within a broader structural context underpinning suffering' an issue that is most pressing in the context of Palestine when we consider Israel's ongoing settler colonial mission, one that oscillates between outright attempts at elimination and erasure, through to an accompanying slow, insidious, and utterly destructive structural violence. Reynolds and Xavier (2016: 975) further note that the narrow focus of ICJ being on individuals and those identified as key actors who bear ultimate overall responsibility for heinous acts 'forecloses the field's ability to tackle the more structural implications of colonisation - from the fragmentation of indigenous communities and the line-drawing of unnatural boundaries to the othering of racialized communities in public discourse'. If we accept these to be fair criticisms, then by extension it is possible to argue that TJ's promotion of this form of top-down retributive 'justice', particularly in areas of ongoing anti-colonial struggle—spaces where there is a pressing need to disrupt, agitate, and radically reform existing structures of power—amounts to a process of conflict management, allowing for individual scapegoats, which can ultimately have a deflating effect overall. None more so is this evident than in the case of Palestine where the role of international law and the international community more broadly—as noted above and throughout—has been to pursue policies of management and control, rather than to support indigenous, anti-colonial modes of resistance.

In the present context, this individualisation of culpability, the process of selectively choosing what crimes are worthy of pursuing for prosecution, further serves to splinter and fragment an already dislocated Palestinian population and creates (inadvertently) a hierarchy of victimhood, a process that in turn damages and detracts from the overarching goal of decolonisation. Moreover, when we consider that 'the creation of the PA was essentially a colonial subcontracting operation, with the Palestinian leadership expected to concern itself with protecting Israeli security' (Collins, 2011: 120), any recourse to the ICC will suffer a legitimacy crisis amongst the Palestinian population if it is led by the PA, those who share a responsibility in propping up the colonial structures that impact upon the Palestinian population. The PAs involvement in joint security cooperation with the colonial power and their determination to quash anti-colonial resistance when it operates in such a way as to undermine their very existence renders them complicit agents and thus, I suggest, unsuitable spokespersons when it comes to delineating the parameters around what amounts to 'justice'. If the ICC is to have emancipatory potential and to be pivoted in service of the Palestinian population, it must be driven by grassroots NGOs, specifically those who are clear on the need for decolonisation and who are not beholden to a two-state fallacy, one that follows the line of the redundant Oslo Accords. Moreover, those who do choose to engage with the machinations of the ICC in pursuit of justice must ensure that they centre the language of decolonisation at every opportunity.

Conclusion

The decision to turn towards the ICC may be seen as a pragmatic approach by Palestine's political elite, with Reynolds and Xavier (2016: 976) suggesting that perhaps it represents a widespread belief that there exists 'a lack of viable emancipatory alternatives' and a perception amongst some 'old timers' who are worn out and who believe the 'heyday of Third World national liberationism' has long since been and gone. Others are less pessimistic and argue that 'top-down' engagement with the international organs such as the ICC may be useful in spurring on, 'third party states, companies, and international organizations to review their engagements with Israeli entities and ensure that they do not give legal effect to unlawful Israeli conduct' (Azarova, 2015). However, 'Decolonisation', as Halper (2021: 125) reminds us, 'may have the moral backing of international law, but it remains an issue to be fought out just as it was in Fanon's time'. The turn towards the ICC is a significant moment in time; however, the likelihood of any potential court intervention leading to a fundamental revaluation of Zionist settler colonial activity that has, for the most part, been allowed to continue unabated is highly unlikely. More concerningly, there is a high probability that Palestinian engagement with the ICC will ultimately have the effect of sharpening a focus on Palestinian resistance and drawing a false equivalency between that and Zionist settler colonial violence, an issue that should be given serious consideration, particularly when one takes on board international law's historic and continued blind spot in the region.

'In order to serve an emancipatory function' as Erakat (2019: 4) reminds us 'the law must be wielded in the sophisticated service of a political movement that can give both meaning to the law and also directly challenge the structure of power that has placed Palestinians outside the law'. However, there is no decolonial future in, or for, Palestine that maintains the current hegemonic position and operational structures that currently prop up the PA. Far from being the moves of a sophisticated political movement, the PA's turn towards the ICC is the actions of an organisation determined to retain its relevance and position of power in a time that has long since passed. Given this reality, Palestinians must summon sources of power beyond the existing international and legal structures, if they are to be effective (Halper, 2021: 127). Thankfully, the presence of a vibrant and growing Palestinian civil society, with its transnational connections to other sites of anti-colonial struggle and genuinely transformative platforms for anti-colonial resistance, gives hope that the summoning of new sources of power is taking place. The promotion of this form of top-down TJ intervention chimes with other forms of liberal peacebuilding practice and as such is about containment and control, rather than decolonial justice.

REFERENCES

Abunimah, A. (2006). *One country: A bold proposal to end the Israeli-Palestinian impasse*. Macmillan.
Adem, S. H. (2019). *Historical and political background of the Israeli-Palestinian conflict* (pp. 11–48). Springer.
Azarova, V. (2015, April 1). Palestine's day in court? The unexpected effects of ICC action. *al-Shabaka, 8*.
Azarova, V., & Mariniello, T. (2017). Why the ICC needs a "Palestine situation" (more than Palestine needs the ICC): On the court's potential role(s) in the Israeli-Palestinian context. *Diritti umani e diritto internazionale, 1*, 115–150.
Bisharat, G., et al. (2018). Mobilizing international law in the Palestinian struggle for justice. *Global Jurist, 18*(3).
Bracka, J. (2021). A false messiah? The ICC in Israel/Palestine and the limits of International Criminal Justice. *Vanderbilt Journal of Transnational Law, 54*, 283.
Cavanaugh, K. A. (2002). Selective justice: The case of Israel and the occupied territories. *Fordham International Law Journal, 26*, 934.
Collins, J. M. (2011). *Global Palestine*. Hurst Publishers.
Dugard, J., & Reynolds, J. (2013). Apartheid, international law, and the occupied Palestinian territory. *European Journal of International Law, 24*(3), 867–913.
Erakat, N. (2019). *Justice for some: Law and the question of Palestine*. Stanford University Press.
Falk, R. A. (2017). *Palestine's horizon: Toward a just peace*. Pluto Press.
Halper, J. (2021). *Decolonizing Israel, liberating Palestine: Zionism, settler colonialism, and the case for one democratic state*. Pluto Press.
Hansen, T. O. (2019). Opportunities and challenges seeking accountability for war crimes in Palestine under the International Criminal Court's complementarity regime. *Notre Dame Journal of International & Comparative Law, 9*, 1.
Imseis, A. (2020). Negotiating the illegal: On the United Nations and the illegal occupation of Palestine, 1967–2020. *European Journal of International Law, 31*(3), 1055–1085.

Kearney, M. (2020). Palestine and the International Criminal Court: Asking the right question. In *Contemporary issues facing the International Criminal Court* (pp. 25–38). Brill Nijhoff.

Kearney, M., & Reynolds, J. (2013). Palestine and the politics of international criminal justice. In *The Ashgate research companion to International Criminal Law: Critical perspectives* (pp. 407–434). Ashgate.

McAuliffe, P., & Schwöbel-Patel, C. (2018). Disciplinary matchmaking: Critics of international criminal law meet critics of liberal peacebuilding. *Journal of International Criminal Justice, 16*(5), 985–1009.

Mutua, M. (2000). What is TWAIL? *Proceedings of the ASIL Annual Meeting, 94*, 31–38.

Mutua, M. (2016). *Human rights standards: Hegemony, law, and politics*. SUNY Press.

Osiel, M. J. (2015). 'Transitional justice' in Israel/Palestine? Symbolism and materialism in reparations for mass violence. Ethics and International Affairs. https://www.ethicsandinternationalaffairs.org/2015/transitional-justice-in-israelpalestine-symbolism-and-materialism-in-reparations-for-mass-violence/

Panepinto, A. (2014). Transitional justice: International criminal law and beyond. *Archivio Penale, 3*.

Perugini, N., & Gordon, N. (2015). *The human right to dominate*. Oxford University Press.

Qato, M., & Rabie, K. (2013). Against the law. *Jacobin Magazine, 21*.

Reynolds, J. (2016). Disrupting civility: Amateur intellectuals, international lawyers and TWAIL as praxis. *Third World Quarterly, 37*(11), 2098–2118.

Reynolds, J., & Xavier, S. (2016). 'The dark corners of the world': TWAIL and International Criminal Justice. *Journal of International Criminal Justice, 14*(4), 959–983.

Turner, M. (2015). Peacebuilding as counterinsurgency in the occupied Palestinian territory. *Review of International Studies, 41*(1), 73.

CHAPTER 5

Conclusion

Abstract By situating transitional justice as an extension of other flawed peacebuilding interventions in Palestine, my aim throughout this book has been to challenge scholars to consider more critically for whom such interventions are best served. In highlighting some of the challenges and limitations pertaining to truth recovery that takes place amidst the backdrop of ongoing settler colonialism, I have demonstrated the various ways it can amount to narrative control and damage limitation, rather than acting as a catalyst for change. In unpacking the myriad ways that international law has been weaponised against the Palestinians, I have sought to reaffirm the notes of caution that have long been sounded regarding any possible justice to be gleaned from the outworking of the ICC. Finally, in unpacking how TJ has been warmly embraced by the Israeli academy, here I highlight some of the limitations and restrictions I foresee in relation to the further marginalisation of Palestinian voices and calls for decolonisation as the discipline continues to flourish within the academic apparatus of the settler community.

Keywords Radicalised · Decolonisation · Academic · Reparations

© The Author(s), under exclusive license to Springer Nature Switzerland AG 2023
B. C. Browne, *Transitional (in)Justice and Enforcing the Peace on Palestine*, Rethinking Peace and Conflict Studies,
https://doi.org/10.1007/978-3-031-25394-2_5

> If you stick a knife in my back nine inches and pull it out six inches, there's no progress. If you pull it all the way out that's not progress. Progress is healing the wound that the blow made.
>
> Malcolm X

Introduction

Those whose scholarly and activist work has been focused on realising a decolonised Palestine will be fully aware of the limitations and pitfalls associated with TJ as a mode of peacebuilding intervention, for many (if not all) of the reasons spotlighted in previous chapters. Uncritical promotion of a TJ discourse and praxis in Palestine, born in Western societies where there exists a legacy of settler colonialism and unaddressed justice issues, has the potential to enforce a status quo that is premised on Palestinian acquiescence, the guiding principle underpinning other peacebuilding intrusions to date. Whilst it remains to be seen if TJ interventions will be promoted more vigorously moving forward, should scholars and practitioners who do so avoid platforming conversations that centre on a need for decolonisation and an end to (and reversal of) Zionist settler colonialism, they will only ever be considered partial and ineffective. The time is long overdue for a genuine problematising of TJs role in this context so as to ensure that the 'orthodox transitional justice paradigm' that has been promoted to date can be challenged and disrupted. However, when we take into consideration the sub-disciplines 'fundamentally liberal... origins' (Park, 2020: 265) and the involvement of powerful elites acting as TJ cheerleaders and sponsors across the region, the extent to which this will be possible remains to be seen. Everyday violence, including actual, structural, and economic, against the Indigenous Palestinian population continues (Masalha, 2012) unabated, and Zionism's expanded settler colonial mission has become embedded by a simultaneously impotent and complicit international community. It is against this backdrop that TJ interventions have attempted to take root. However, by their failure to prioritise conversation around decolonisation in Palestine, such strategies often fall short, and as a result, serious questions must be asked regarding specifically at what stage 'should transitional justice be 'turned away' from?' (Park, 2020: 276).

Those who are inoculated from the everyday realities of the scourge of Zionist settler colonialism in Palestine, including international scholars, have a role to play in this regard; however, it is not to set the parameters around what amounts to a practical process of decolonisation. In working intentionally towards ensuring that justice remains a focal point during any transition towards Palestinian liberation, our role is to use positions of privilege and academic freedom to foster deeper engagement with some of the critiques around TJs foundations, so as to spark debate around its colonial overtones. In blending more dutifully our dual role as academic and activist when it comes to justice in Palestine, we should be guided by the words and actions of veteran Black civil rights campaigner and long-term supporter of Palestinian liberation Angela Davis (2016: 145) who reminds us that: 'We cannot go on as usual. We cannot pivot the center. We cannot be moderate. We will have to be willing to stand up and say no with combined spirits, our collective intellects, and our many bodies'. The recent intellectual turn towards considering the suitability of TJ in other settler colonial contexts is a welcome one and the desire for 'radicalisation' (Park, 2020) of the field opens up possible routes for generating a new form of 'transnational transitional justice', one that has at its focal point the needs and voices of Indigenous communities, those who will ultimately be involved in growing and developing the strategies required to transition towards decolonisation. Therefore, if we are genuinely invested in 'radicalising' TJ, as scholars and pedagogues, we must constantly evaluate our craft and focus on how best to ensure the curation of intellectual spaces in the classroom that allow for proper debate and a challenging of long-established TJ boundaries. We must avoid reproducing TJ orthodoxies by importing strategies and techniques from other 'post-conflict' or 'transitional' societies, those that have purportedly worked, into a context that is vastly different. Instead, if we are committed to TJ as a means of shifting on-the-ground realities, we must find better ways of supporting the expanding network of 'grassroots' and community-driven decolonial programmes, those that are already well established.

In seeking to arrive at a suitable conclusion, rather than rehashing arguments that have come before, it is my intention to briefly consider two final issues that I believe are important. In predicting the likelihood that TJ in the present context will become more vociferously championed and practised by a diverse range of actors—including 'peace' practitioners, international organisations, and academics—I wish to draw particular attention to the way that the sub-discipline has been embedded within the bosom of the Israeli academy, the supposed last bastion of Israeli liberalism. This, I suggest, is an area worth highlighting when we take into consideration issues related to control around growth of the liberal language and intellectual growth of TJ as a mode of peacebuilding intervention. Finally, in considering whether or not to dispense with TJ altogether, I wish to centre Park's (2020) work on the issue of a 'radicalised' TJ and in the context of Palestine ask what any 'radicalisation' ultimately would entail. In so doing I argue that, should those who choose to engage in TJ practice in this context fully embrace the language of decolonisation, then perhaps there is a possibility that the justice issues that have emerged as a result of Zionism's settler colonial mission in Palestine will be given a more suitable platform. Thus, far from providing definitive conclusions, my aim here is to open up a conversation that allows for a sharpening of scholarly focus pertaining to TJs suitability when it comes to providing a meaningful decolonial justice in and for Palestine.

Liberalising 'Justice' Through the Israeli Academy: Why Who Speaks, Matters

The links between the Israeli academy and the outworking of Zionism's settler colonial mission in historic Palestine have been long documented, and are carefully detailed on the website of the Palestinian Campaign for the Academic and Cultural Boycott of Israel (PACBI):

> For decades, Israeli universities have played a key role in planning, implementing, and justifying Israel's occupation and apartheid policies, while maintaining a uniquely close relationship with the Israeli military. Tel Aviv University, for example, has developed tens of weapon systems and the "Dahiya doctrine" of disproportionate force employed by the Israeli military in committing war crimes against Palestinian and Lebanese civilians.

PACBI note the role that certain aspects of the Israeli academy play when it comes to the control and attempted erasure of the Palestinian population, including by providing the technological and intellectual expertise required to manufacture high-grade military weapons trialled on the Palestinian population under siege in the Gaza Strip, and designing the security infrastructure associated with the Israeli 'Separation Barrier', developed in conjunction with academics at the Technion, Israel Institute of Technology, Haifa. Israeli universities remain spaces deeply hostile to Palestinian identity, culture, and heritage, and in providing willing intellectual accomplices, they retain a position as a constituent element in Zionism's ongoing settler colonial mission in historic Palestine. Palestinian students attending Israeli campuses routinely face discrimination and anti-Palestinian abuse. In May 2022, an attempt at quashing Palestinian student dissent and demonstration was brought before the Israeli Knesset by way of a bill which proposed a complete prohibition on the displaying of Palestinian flags and identifiers on Israeli campuses, a decision made all the more ludicrous when you consider the very fact that just under 2 million Palestinians live within the 1948 borders. Palestinian universities are routinely subjected to Israeli attempts at suppression (as the preface to this book has outlined), with direct attacks against the Palestinian academy having a long and brutal history. During the first Intifada, all Palestinian universities were shuttered between 1987 and 1993. In 2014, the Islamic University in Gaza (IUG) was completely destroyed following an attack by Israeli war planes. According to PACBI, Israeli academics working at Israeli universities therefore become complicit actors in this suppression of Palestinian academic freedom by their failure to speak out and stand in solidarity as a collective against the actions of their state whilst such events are unfolding, providing a veneer of respectability for the Israeli occupation, and materially assisting in providing the practical and intellectual apparatus for the expansion of the attempted erasure of the Indigenous Palestinian population.

In recent years, scholarly activity in a number of Israeli universities (perhaps somewhat predictably when you consider the far reaching, international appeal of the discipline) has turned to consider TJ as a mode of peacebuilding intervention. The result has been the burgeoning growth of TJ pedagogy and research developed by a hybrid mix of Israeli (and some leading international) TJ scholars, including those who would be considered foremost 'experts' in the field. When we consider the close ties between the Israeli academy and the Israeli state (as noted above), this turn towards an intellectual embedding of TJ by those who hold prominent access to seats of power, including academics working in the university sector, should spark our interest. 'Speaking for and about victims' as Madlingozi (2010: 210) reminds us 'perpetuates their disempowerment and marginality', and as such, the embedded nature of TJ within the Israeli academy raises significant questions relating to the manner in which Palestinian loss, suffering, erasure, and entitlement to justice is being curated and restricted through the apparatus of the Israeli academy, an extension of the Israeli state that has a history of producing intellectual work which has served to further marginalise the Palestinian subaltern (Spivak, 1988). Academic work in every society drives policy decisions and helps embed a dominant narrative. When it comes to promoting TJ in Israel, this invariably results in the fostering of an orthodoxy around TJ that replicates, consolidates, and delineates specific values, views, and positions around what amounts to 'transition' and 'justice' in and for Palestine and Palestinians. Given the almost 'complete hegemonic coalescence between the liberal Western view of things and the Zionist - Israeli view' (Said, 1980: 37), and when set alongside the utterly destructive outworking of the peacebuilding framework as has been applied in the present context (as noted in Chapter 2), this academic embrace of TJ education and research is perhaps unsurprising.

Despite being one of the most heavily researched areas on the planet, many international scholars who choose to focus on TJ in other settings have eschewed a critical analysis of how it operates in the Palestine-Israeli context (with a few notable exceptions). As such, the pool of critical literature upon which to draw conclusions is relatively sparse. The reasons for this can be speculated upon, however, one could argue that fear of institutional rebuke holds some back, whilst others are working in TJ institutions who have well-established connections with Israeli academic institutions (usually through Law schools) and are perhaps less inclined or unwilling to rock the often lucrative (in terms of grant access and career progression) boat. Given Palestine and Palestinians have (problematically) long been spoken about, spoken for, and analysed as subjects rather than individuals with agency, this engagement in, what I consider to be academic self-censorship, speaks volumes in and of itself. I therefore contend that, by becoming further embedded within the Israeli university sector, and being relatively unchallenged by scholars who work on TJ in other global hot spots, the discipline has been given fertile ground to grow, develop, and thus demarcate the parameters around what amounts to 'transition' and 'justice' across the region.

TRANSITIONAL JUSTICE IN THE ISRAELI ACADEMY: MAPPING THE FIELD

The incremental growth of TJ in Israeli academic institutions has involved, *inter alia*, the development of educational programmes that focus on TJ (at both undergraduate and postgraduate levels), establishment of TJ centres of excellence, forging of international partnerships between Israeli institutions and universities located in other supposedly 'post-conflict/transitional' spaces, and the hosting of international conferences that bring world renowned experts to Israeli institutions to share academic views on TJ best practice. All of this academic work has helped to foster the emergence of a TJ orthodoxy within the Israeli academy, with the vast majority of these TJ activities funnelled through Israel's largest and top-ranked universities, Tel Aviv University, and the Hebrew University in Jerusalem. A sizeable chunk of this TJ intellectual work that takes place within the Israeli academy is funded by The Minerva Stiftung, a German organisation founded in 1962, with the stated aim of establishing German-Israeli cooperation. It does so by establishing centres of excellence (24 to date, the first being established in 1975) and takes as its focus emerging research fields which are 'not yet well established in Israel and which does not yet attract sufficient grants and donations'. The organisation in turn receives financial support from the German Federal Ministry for Education and Research (BMBF). The largest project pertaining to TJ specifically is the establishment of the Minerva Centre for Human Rights, a joint Tel Aviv University/Hebrew University in Jerusalem project established across both sites in 1995 to 'promote interest in human rights issues in the academic community and at large'. Under the auspices of the centre, in 2014 (the same year Israel launched its genocidal assault on the Gaza Strip) a specific TJ programme was launched with aims to 'promote education, research, conferences and academic collaborations in the interdisciplinary field of transitional justice, with an emphasis on the Israeli-Palestinian conflict'. Building on the intellectual energy around this joint collaboration, the Hebrew University in Jerusalem embarked upon the development of specific courses on TJ, including a full MA on Human Rights and Transitional Justice, and several undergraduate courses entitled: Transitional Justice Colloquium: Comparative Jurisprudential and Regional Perspectives (led by the founder of TJ, Prof. Ruti Teitel); Introduction to Transitional Justice; and Transitional Justice in Israel. The latter course seeks to introduce students to issues such as: 'Transitional justice and the Holocaust; the Yemenite children's affair; East Jerusalem; the unrecognized Bedouin villages in the Negev; and the disengagement plan'. Alongside these pedagogical interventions, a swathe of international capacity building events, including conferences and international study trips, have been initiated, including 'lesson learning' events in Northern Ireland.

One of the foundational voices of the sub-discipline, Prof. Ruti Teitel has become a central figure in leading on Israel's TJ expansion, specifically at the Hebrew University of Jerusalem, where she established the Fried Gal Colloquium (with support from the Gal foundation) to 'explore TJ from international, comparative, and regional perspectives'. Since 2012, the Fried Gal Colloquium has platformed a number of high-profile events, including hosting a lecture series involving international TJ experts, many of whom have covered issues related to TJ in other global hot spots. Teitel's work on TJ remains consistently amongst the most highly cited internationally and (as noted before) she is credited with being the founding voice of the sub-discipline. For anyone interested in the emergence of TJ, her book 'Transitional Justice' (Teitel, 2000) is the definitive 'go to' source for academics and practitioners alike, with over 3300 citations (at the time of writing). Her appointment in spearheading the growth and development of TJ within the Hebrew University of Jerusalem is therefore a major coup. The Mount Scopus Campus of the Hebrew University of Jerusalem is physically located on occupied land and thus inaccessible to the vast majority of Palestinians, including all who live in the West Bank, Gaza Strip, and wider diaspora and who are refused the requisite 'permission' from the Israeli authorities to enter East Jerusalem. Therefore, the emergence of a TJ programme, led by the leading voice in the discipline, that seeks to interrogate issues relating to 'transition' and 'justice' in Palestine/Israel, that takes place in an area where the voices of the oppressed are considered unwelcome, is, I suggest, the supreme example of settler colonial narrative control, and further evidence of TJs facilitative role in seeking to contain and delineate what is viewed as acceptable. Embedding TJ programmes in spaces where the coloniser has a monopoly over the language, discourse, and framing of issues supposedly related to 'justice'—those that have direct implications for the colonised—and by availing of the support of powerful international allies, including experts who have not heeded the PACBI call to avoid practices that normalise relationships with a violent settler colonial state practising policies of systematic apartheid and attempted erasure of the native population, speaks volumes about TJs liberal foundations.

In noting that 'Colonialism… is a formation of discourse and as an operation of discourse it interpellates colonial subjects by incorporating them in a system of representation' (Tiffin & Lawson, 1994: 3), when it comes to curating conversations around 'transition' and 'justice' against the backdrop of expanding Zionist settler colonialism in Palestine, Palestinians remain objects of TJ enquiry, rather than engaged actors, with legitimate decolonial aspirations. The role the Israeli academy has assumed in helping to embed the fabric of Zionist settler colonialism in Palestine has extended into the realms of TJ, which, rather than seeking to redress and reverse, has instead served to further embed deep asymmetrical power imbalances. TJ in its current iteration remains safely cocooned in the bosom of the fully complicit Israeli academy and with useful cheerleaders, has germinated in such a way as to become a figleaf used to soften the edges of the violent reality of the Zionist settler colonial project, promoting (as it does) a language and narrative that sits well within the broader (deeply flawed) peacebuilding framework. This, I maintain, is the very essence of what amounts to transitional (in)justice.

Conclusion: Can TJ Be 'Radicalised'?

'Settler colonialism' as has been noted by Collins (2011: 50) 'is a political creature that refuses to speak its own name'. In failing to embrace the language of 'settler colonialism', TJ interventions that take place in such contexts promote stability and normalisation of deeply violent environments, rather than agitating for decolonisation, through advocating for the guise of 'justice' for a few determined persons via 'softer mechanisms'. Rather than throwing the baby out with the bath water, and dismiss TJs suitability in the present context altogether, it is worth considering if TJ would benefit from a process of 'radicalisation' (Park, 2020) before reaching any final conclusion. Given its liberal foundations and the role played by international organisations most vociferous in developing its burgeoning appeal as a mode of peacebuilding, a 'radicalised' TJ in sites of historic and ongoing settler colonialism could simply be interpreted as a mode of practice that actively promotes the need for decolonisation. The very fact that there is a perceived need for TJ to undergo a 'radical' turn is revelatory in and of itself in that it further demonstrates the fact that, for many Indigenous communities, the justice component of TJ has long been conspicuous by its absence. In this sense, what is 'radical' is the departure from TJs foundations as a practice trialled (and often imposed) in post-colonial sites. A decolonial justice framework would then be one based on the needs and recommendations of the Indigenous community, those who have borne, or continue to experience, settler colonial violence.

Up until this point existing TJ practice (Rolston & Ní Aoláin, 2018) has been somewhat limited when it comes to engaging in addressing colonial injustices, with Nagy (2022: 191) arguing that 'redressing colonial injustice remains at the 'margins of accountability' within transitional justice'. Moreover, it is far from conspiratorial to suggest that TJ routinely acts as a method of 'settler colonial self-suppression' (Park, 2020: 268) allowing for a 'line in the sand' between a period of foundational, colonial violence and the 'settled' present. In this sense, its utility could be considered nefarious, allowing for the cursory consideration of a select number of justice issues, giving the appearance of being seen to be 'doing something' whilst effectively avoiding the need to fully engage with a process of decolonisation, one that invariably presents far more practical challenges and difficulties for those who enjoy a privileged status amidst the protective embrace of the settler state. If it is ever (at all) considered, 'The question of decolonization' according to Collins (2011: 139) is usually met with 'outright denial... or through highly circumscribed processes of reconciliation that do little to alter deeper colonial hierarchies'. Therefore, and in rehashing a central tenant that runs throughout this book, the question for those who remain committed to TJ having a role in aiding peacebuilding in spaces of ongoing settler colonial violence is: how do we ensure that TJ aids decolonisation, or, to return to Roberts (2020) how do we ensure that TJ interventions are not 'colonised'?

Critical scholarly work by both Park (2020) and Nagy (2022) has separately provided the most significant contributions to date on the debate surrounding TJ's limitations when it comes to facilitating decolonisation, and in considering whether transformative justice interventions might offer up more concrete solutions to addressing Indigenous concerns. In her analysis of the role of TJ in the context of settled, settler democracies, Park (2020) maintains that a 'radicalised' TJ would involve redefining the relationship between traditional TJ interventions and the apparatus of the state, thus ensuring that Indigenous structures and practices receive primacy. She further argues:

> Radicalized transitional justice would abandon liberal teleology, recognizing the deep interrelation between liberalism and settler colonialism. As we have seen in the decolonizing refusal of the politics of recognition and the resurgence of Indigenous traditions, liberalism is decidedly not the future proposed by the Indigenous scholars... At the same time, refusing

teleological rationality *tout court* disrupts the settler's linear concept of time and the colonial ideology of progress. (Park, 2020: 279)

Building upon this argument further, Park (2020: 279) spotlights opportunities that may exist for a 'radicalisation' of the field, suggesting that by 'Reading paradigmatic cases through the lens of settler colonialism and decolonization' we may be able to gain 'new insights into the limitations (and promise) of transitional justice for Indigenous peoples'. Similarly, in 'contributing an indigenised, decolonial account of transformative justice in a settler colonial transition', Nagy (2022: 192) has provided a framework upon which to build, particularly for those who retain a belief in pursuing TJ interventions in other settler colonial contexts. Whilst it doesn't map directly on to the current context of Palestine's encounter with Zionist settler colonialism, the radical TJ turn that both Park (2020) and Nagy (2022) advocate mirrors much of the decolonial thinking that has been advanced by Palestinian scholars and their allies. However, rather than re-evaluating and seeking to provide justice by repairing the relationship between the Indigenous Palestinian population and the Israeli state, it is crucial to remember that in terms of decolonisation in Palestine, 'There is no just solution that does not travel through a direct confrontation with Israel's insistence upon maintaining Jewish sovereignty and the framework of exception that has made that sovereignty an immovable priority' (Erakat, 2019: 237). Similarly, as Halper (2021: 138) has argued, when it comes to thinking of creative solutions to advance the cause of Palestinian liberation, 'we cannot forfeit the truth - in this case the fact of Zionist settler colonialism - simply to render "peace-making" easier'. Therefore, TJ interventions, as extensions of a peacebuilding praxis, if they are to have any legitimacy, cannot shirk this reality for the sake of political expediency. Those who champion TJ in the present context must sharpen their language and speak more directly and intentionally to this fundamental, underlying root cause of 'conflict', for far from being an 'academic exercise' (Halper, 2021: 186) the reframing allows for a more justice-oriented discussion pertaining to the ultimate end goal, namely a reversal of Zionist settler colonialism and a decolonised Palestine premised on the need for repair.

Attentive to warnings platformed by decolonial scholars, including Tuck and Yang (2012), any TJ interventions proposed as an aid to decolonisation must not be reduced to a metaphor, and:

must involve the repatriation of land simultaneous to the recognition of how land and relations to land have always already been differently understood and enacted, that is all of the land and not just symbolically. (Tuck & Yang, 2012: 5)

Translated into the context of Palestine, the only logical conclusion to be reached is that TJ interventions, if they are proposed, must engage meaningfully in conversations around 'land back' if they are to avoid the charge of being 'liberal, interventionist irrelevance' (Browne, 2021). To be sure, such decolonial conversations have always happened within and across Palestinian communities (AbuNimah, 2006; Baroud & Pappé, 2022), and as a result, there is much groundwork done already upon which those who retain hope in the possibility of TJ in this context could build upon. Arguments around return have long been central when it comes to realising a decolonial future in Palestine; however, to date, they too have been subjected to internal and international interference, including various attempts at containment and control for the sake of chasing a two-state fallacy based on Palestinian concession. Therefore, if it is to avoid the charge of being a facilitator of settler colonial erasure in Palestine and an extension of the flawed peacebuilding apparatus, TJ must seek to 'unsettle colonial hierarchies' to borrow from Collins (2011: 139). The challenge therefore for those who advocate its usage is to ensure that it seeks ways of disrupting and undermining the dominant Zionist settler state-sponsored narrative rather than allowing for its unchecked expansion. At the same time, TJ interventions must ensure that justice remains the focal point during the pursuit of realisation of a decolonial moment. In so doing, it must ensure that it is the voices of those who have borne the brunt of Zionist settler colonialism who are afforded primacy in terms of leading these legitimate justice demands.

In helping to envisage a just, decolonised Palestine, an area that is ripe for more focused intellectual and practical work is the careful consideration of what may be considered future reparations for victims of Zionist settler colonialism. Genuine decolonial reparatory justice, if it is to be viewed as sustainable and legitimate in the eyes of the Indigenous community, must not be premised on the need for Indigenous compromise, as has been the guiding principle during the various peacebuilding interventions trialled thus far since the foundation of Israeli state in 1948. In referencing the language of the UN, Khoury (2021: 159) points to the fact that the language around reparations encompasses a variety of issues, including (and most pertinently in the context of Palestine) 'restituting original property to refugees, aiding their return, ending ongoing violations, holding perpetrators accountable, commemorating the victims, acknowledging wrongs, issuing a public apology, and implementing a variety of measures to prevent the reoccurrence of injustice'. All of which is nothing short of ironic when we consider the role the UN has played when it comes to marginalising the rights of Palestinian refugees to date. Therefore, those who are perhaps less inclined to call for a 'radicalisation' of TJ, or who withdraw from the language of settler colonialism, could simply advocate for and work towards full implementation of the principles of international law that are supposed to govern inter-state relations and work on behalf of victims and survivors. Hardly all that radical!

Beyond the idea of individualised reparations for victims and survivors, and when we consider the underlying logic of Zionist settler colonialism as being an attempt to erase an Indigenous presence on the land and replace it with a 'new' settled community, decolonial reparations in this context would also amount to a process of repair that strengthens Palestinian connection with the land. Practical steps that will require consideration include the process of demobilisation of a violent settler colonial architecture, the infrastructure of which has sought to forge a disconnect between Indigenous Palestinian communities and the land itself. Whilst this most obviously includes the removal of the illegal Israeli 'Separation Barrier', militarised checkpoints, and associated barriers, it also requires the disbanding of illegal Israeli settlements across the West Bank and East Jerusalem and the associated infrastructure that has been developed to serve the settler community. To be sure, repair in the long term will also require a process of relational rebuilding, reunification between, and across the various communities who inhabit the land. However, attempts to do so in advance of a full reversal of the Zionist settler colonial project, one that is predicated on Jewish supremacy and Palestinian subjugation, will be fundamentally flawed.

By situating TJ as an extension of other flawed peacebuilding interventions and as being a set of socio-political and ideological mechanisms designed to sustain the status quo of colonial Israel in a systematic way at the expense of the existential reality of historic Palestine, my aim throughout this book has been to challenge TJ scholars to consider more critically for whom such interventions are best served. In demonstrating some of the challenges and limitations pertaining to truth recovery that takes place amidst the backdrop of ongoing settler colonialism, I have revealed the various ways it can amount to narrative control and damage limitation, rather than acting as a catalyst for change. In unpacking the myriad ways that international law has been weaponised against the Palestinians, I have sought to reaffirm the notes of caution that have long been sounded regarding any possible justice to be gleaned from the outworking of the ICC. Finally, in unpacking how TJ has been warmly embraced by the Israeli academy, I have sought to highlight some of the limitations and restrictions I foresee in relation to the further marginalisation of Palestinian voices and calls for decolonisation as the discipline continues to flourish within the academic apparatus of the settler community. The recent scholarly turn towards considering the role of TJ in other settler colonial contexts opens up interesting possibilities for transnational solidarity, particularly around fostering Indigenous modes of best practice that are not 'colonised' (Roberts, 2020) by external actors. In connecting Palestine to other sites of Indigenous struggle, it is possible to generate more joined up thinking around how to 'radicalise' TJ. Similarly, in reflecting on the ways in which a 'decolonial transformative justice' may aid in the 'unsettling of colonial relations through settler decolonisation' (Nagy, 2022: 208), greater emphasis can be placed on fostering a praxis that shifts the onus away from state building and institutional reform, to a TJ that is truly grassroots driven and one that prioritises the voices of Indigenous communities over international interventionists.

If it is to have any role to play in the context of realising a decolonised Palestine, TJ scholarship and praxis must prioritise conversations on decolonial justice as a precursor to any future peace. There can be no softening of the sharp edges of Zionist settler colonialism and so those who most vociferously champion TJ as a mode of peacebuilding intervention must learn to find their voice and to define the reality on the ground clearly, and without obfuscation. Failure to do so is not only intellectually spurious, it allows for the maintenance of a dangerous everyday reality that defines the relationship between colonised and coloniser. Promotion of soft TJ interventions in and for Palestine that remain silent when it comes to legitimate decolonial demands run afoul of the charge of tokenism, the very essence of what amounts to transitional (in)justice. As such, what they aim for and ultimately promote can only ever be considered partial and incomplete.

References

Abunimah, A. (2006). *One country: A bold proposal to end the Israeli-Palestinian impasse*. Macmillan.
Baroud, R., & Pappé, I. (2022). *Our vision for liberation. Engaged Palestinian leaders and intellectuals speak out*. Clarity Press.
Browne, B. C. (2021). Disrupting settler-colonialism or enforcing the liberal 'peace'? Transitional (in) justice in Palestine-Israel. *Journal of Holy Land and Palestine Studies*, *20*(1), 1–27.
Collins, J. M. (2011). *Global Palestine*. Hurst Publishers.
Davis, A. Y. (2016). *Freedom is a constant struggle: Ferguson, Palestine, and the foundations of a movement*. Haymarket Books.
Erakat, N. (2019). *Justice for some: Law and the question of Palestine*. Stanford University Press.
Halper, J. (2021). *Decolonizing Israel, liberating Palestine: Zionism, Settler colonialism, and the case for one democratic state*. Pluto Press.
Khoury, N. (2021). Transitional justice in Palestine/Israel: Whose justice? Which transition? In L. Farsakh (Ed.), *Rethinking statehood in Palestine*. University of California Press. https://doi.org/10.1525/luminos.113.g
Madlingozi, T. (2010). On transitional justice entrepreneurs and the production of victims. *Journal of Human Rights Practice*, *2*(2), 208–228.
Masalha, N. (2012). *The Palestine Nakba: Decolonising history, narrating the subaltern, reclaiming memory*. Zed Books.
Nagy, R. (2022). Transformative justice in a settler colonial transition: Implementing the UN Declaration on the Rights of Indigenous Peoples in Canada. *The International Journal of Human Rights*, *26*(2), 191–216.
Park, A. S. J. (2020). Settler colonialism, decolonization and radicalizing transitional justice. *International Journal of Transitional Justice*, *14*(2), 260–279. https://doi.org/10.1093/ijtj/ijaa006
Roberts, R. S. (2020). How 'transitional justice' colonized SouthAfrica's TRC. *Modern Languages Open*, *34*(1), 1–15.
Rolston, B., & Ní Aoláin, F. (2018). Colonialism, redress and transitional justice: Ireland and beyond. *State Crime Journal*, *7*(2), 329–348.
Said, E. (1980). Islam through western eyes. *The Nation*, *26*(1), 14–18.
Spivak, G. S. (1988). Can the subaltern speak? In C. Nelson & L. Grossberg (Eds.), *Marxism and the interpretation of culture*. University of Illinois Press.
Teitel, R. G. (2000). *Transitional justice*. Oxford University Press on Demand.
Tiffin, C., & Lawson, A. (Eds.). (1994). *De-scribing empire: Post-colonialism and textuality*. Taylor & Francis.
Tuck, E., & Yang, K. W. (2012). Decolonization is not a metaphor. *Decolonization: Indigeneity, Education & Society*, *1*(1), 1–40.

Index

A
Academic institutions, 84
Accountability, 51
Activist work, 80
Advent of globalisation, 28
Advisory Opinions, 65
Anti-colonial resistance, 66
Anti-colonial struggle, 14
Apartheid, 9
Asymmetry, 35

B
Balfour, Arthur, 30

C
Cartography, 51
Catastrophic fragmentation, 67
Colonial, 6
Colonialism, 7
Colonised/Colonized, 3, 14
Confession without consequence, 46
Conflict, 2

Convergence, 28
Counter-narratives, 43

D
Decolonisation, 44
Deterring future war crimes, 63
Dignity, 26
Discourse, 86
Donors, 33

E
Educational programmes, 84
Elimination, 48
Eurocentric ideology, 24
Exceptionalist, 73
Exile, 31

F
Fateh, 34
Formal acknowledgement, 52
Future reparations, 90

G
Genocide, 62
Governmentality, 66
Grassroots, 92
Grievable life, 44

H
Hamas, 34
Hebrew University, 85
Hybrid tribunals, 62

I
Indigenous, 13
Individualisation of culpability, 75
Intellectual apparatus, 83
Interdisciplinarity, 24
International Criminal Court (ICC), 62
International Criminal Justice (ICJ), 62
International law, 64
Interventions, 4
Intifada, 83
Israeli, 34
Israeli academy, 81
Israeli liberalism, 17

J
Jewish people, 30
Joint security, 75
Judaization, 45

L
Language, 5
'Lawfare', 68
Legal models, 67
Liberal bias, 48
Liberal governmentality, 28

M
Mandate Palestine, 50
Margins of accountability, 88
'Memoricide', 45
Minerva Stiftung, 85

N
Nakba, 45

O
On transitional justice and the production of victims, 14
Orthodoxy(ies), 5, 81

P
Palestinian Campaign for the Academic and Cultural Boycott of Israel (PACBI), 82
Palestinian civil society, 76
Palestinian National Authority, 32
Palestinian statehood, 12, 69
Partition, 72
Peacebuilding, 10
Peace processes, 31
Permanent erasure, 25
Permission, 55
Personal victimhood, 71
Policy decisions, 84
Political leverage, 64
Preliminary examination, 69
Prosecution, 62

Q
Question of rights, 74

R
Radicalisation/Radicalization, 8, 81
'Reconciliation', 9

Redress, 27
Refugee, 33
Relational rebuilding, 91
Remember, 54
Reparatory justice, 90
Resistance, 12
Retributive justice, 71
Right of return, 50

S
Settler colonialism, 2
State of Palestine, 32
Structural, 80
Structural violence, 34
Structure of power, 76

T
Technocratic discourse, 48
Teitel, R.G., 86
Third World Approaches to
    International Law (TWAIL), 74

Tokenism, 92
Transformative justice, 89
Transition, 12
Transitional justice (TJ), 2
Transnational appeal, 16
Truth recovery, 42
Truths, 42

U
United Nations (UN), 30

W
War crimes, 54
Weaponised, 67

Z
Zionist, 10, 29
Zochrot, 46

The manufacturer's authorised representative in the EU is Springer Nature Customer Service Centre GmbH, Europaplatz 3, 69115 Heidelberg, Germany. If you have any concerns regarding our products, please contact ProductSafety@springernature.com

Printed and bound by CPI Group (UK) Ltd, Croydon, CR0 4YY

23/03/2026

02076447-0005